D0453756

CLEAN LIVING
IN A DIRTY WORLD

Though this book is designed for group study, it is also intended for your personal enjoyment and spiritual growth. A leader's guide is available from your local bookstore or from your publisher.

Copyright 1991
Beacon Hill Press of Kansas City
Kansas City, Missouri

Printed in the United States of America
ISBN: 083-411-2787

Editor
Stephen M. Miller

Editorial Assistants
Rebecca Privett
Kathryn Roblee

Editorial Committee
Dan Burnett
Thomas Mayse
Stephen M. Miller
Carl Pierce
Gene Van Note
Lyle Williams

Contents

Chapter 1

The Media—Are We Really What We Eat?

by Bill Myers

Background Scripture: Romans 12:1-2; Philippians 4:8

IF YOU'RE LOOKING for a bunch of rules and regulations on what to watch or listen to, forget it. By now we've all heard the horror stories about rock music, TV, and films, so I'm not going to waste your time with a bunch of dos and don'ts.

The decision is yours. You're the guardian of your mind, and what you choose to feed it is up to you.

But as a full-time writer and film director, I'd like to share a little more of what goes on behind the scenes to help you make those decisions.

The Power to Change Us

We're all bombarded by the media. It has become a major factor in most of our lives. In fact, according to a Nielsen survey, today's typical adult logs more time before the screen than in any other activity except sleep.

Other surveys seem to indicate we spend more time absorbing information from the media than we do from our friends, churches, or family. And for this reason many sociologists count the media as *one of the greatest single forces* shaping our lives today.

In fact, a study by J. L. Singer at Yale University states: "The outlook on *any* moral value can be changed through TV viewing." Think of that for a moment. Any moral value you have can be changed through the media. *Any moral value.* Now that's power.

And there's nothing wrong with that type of power, nothing wrong with helping to shape a person's outlook—if it's for the good. But who determines what is good? Not you. Not me. The people who make those decisions are the top executives in charge of the media corporations. Now, many of them are good people with good motives. In fact, according to George Barna and William Paul McKay in their book *Vital Signs* (Crossway), "Two out of three TV executives

---

This chapter has been written by a Christian who is employed in the film industry. He brings a unique perspective to the issue of the media. Though we may not agree with all of his opinions, we feel his warnings, as a film industry insider, are compelling. Our desire is that his advice will encourage readers toward more thoughtful decisions concerning the media we allow ourselves to see. *The Editors*

suggested that television should promote social reform." And, "The select few who have control of the medium are consciously striving to transform American society, through television, to conform to their vision of what is right and desirable."

Like I said, those are great motives. But the problem lies in what *they* consider "right and desirable." Is it the same as what you and I would consider?

To get a better handle on their outlook, here's a survey of some of the top TV executives in the country, as quoted in *Vital Signs:*

- 7 percent of television executives regularly attend church.
- 97 percent are in favor of women having the right to abortion.
- 80 percent feel there is nothing wrong with homo-sexuality.
- 51 percent believe there is nothing wrong with adultery.

Now I don't know about you, but I'm not crazy about people with that moral outlook getting inside my head and trying to "conform" *my* thinking to what *they* consider "right and desirable."

And since many executives look on Christianity as something narrow-minded and repressive, it's doubtful you'll see much of Christ or His principles on the ol' tube.

I know of one Christian in the story department of a major TV series who is constantly putting in references to God and is constantly getting them removed. It's not because the executives are "evil" but because they simply disagree with the Christian concept of God and morality. Of course, my friend can expect the usual excuse, "We just don't want to offend our viewers." (This is always good for a laugh, since no one's concerned about offending when it comes to murder, adultery, and language; but when it comes to mentioning God, everyone suddenly becomes concerned about "offending.")

Anyway, let no one tell you there isn't prejudice in Hollywood. There is. I've experienced it, and so have most of my Christian friends. It's not always conscious, but it is always there. And if you're a Christian, much of it is directed against what you believe.

The Goal: Manipulation

As a writer and director my primary objective is to manipulate you. I'm successful only if I can get you to cry, to laugh, to ache, and to be thrilled exactly when I want you to.

All the years I've trained, all the dialogue I write, every camera angle I choose, and all the music I use is designed for one reason and one reason only: to manipulate your emotions. If I succeed and really grab you, you'll tell all your friends, they'll tell theirs, and suddenly I have a hit. That's the name of the game. And few things feel as good to moviemakers as watching the audience cry when we want them to cry and laugh when we want them to laugh.

Now don't get me wrong; manipulation is not necessarily bad. I like getting caught up in a good story as much as the next guy. All I'm saying is when you step into the theater or turn on the tube, be aware that somebody out there is trying to manipulate you; then decide if that is the picture or show you want to be manipulated by. If it is, fine. If not, pass. Because you will not go away unaffected.

Let me repeat that: *You will not go away unaffected.* We've gotten too good at doing what we do.

And unfortunately, not all professionals in the media use their skills just to entertain or present their view of the world.

Not long ago I knew of a well-known actor that a beer company kept asking to make a commercial. It was a great idea and destined to be a tremendous hit and a classic for years. The offer was very tempting, but because of his new faith in Christ the actor just didn't think he should make it. So the company kept offering him more and more money and the temptation kept growing until, unable to stand any more, he finally went in to see the vice president of the company.

"Why is it so important to you fellows that I make this commercial?" he asked.

The V.P. smiled. "That's easy. Our reports show that you have a strong following of kids from the ages of 9 to 13. We want them."

The actor walked out— he had his answer.

That's just one example. What about the more subtle manipulations that have convinced us to equate fat with failure, love with lust, success with possessions, holiness with narrow-mindedness?

Millions of dollars are spent every year to find out how best to get your attention, to make you feel what we want you to feel, and to make you buy what we want you to buy. In short, all that money is being invested to find out how to pull your strings.

And the same goes for music. I just talked to a guitarist who plays with a superfamous rock star known for his crazy, anything-goes life-style. On stage this superstar will stagger over to a bottle of Jack Daniels and chug down a healthy swig to everyone's cheers and applause. What no one bothers to tell the audience is that it's all a show. A way to grab them and make them believe he's living a wild, reckless, carefree life . . . a life they can also enjoy. No one bothers to tell them they're being lied to and manipulated. No one bothers to tell them that it's Lipton tea inside that bottle.

What Should We Do?

There are the facts. So what do we do with them: Smash the set, boycott the movies, burn the albums?

What you can and should do is be very cautious and very, very selective. It's true, the media's power can be used for good. That's why I and many others are in it. If you can find the good and edifying things, go for it. But if you can't, then stay away. I mean, you've only got one mind. Why let someone get inside and mess it up?

I'm telling you the absolute truth. To this day there are scenes I would literally pay money to have removed from my memory. As it is, they'll stay with me the rest of my life; they will always haunt me, and there's nothing I can do about it.

Television

To be quite frank, if I were not in the business I'm in, I would probably have sold the TV set by now. Granted, there are some excellent shows on from time to time, but I often feel like I'm wading through a garbage dump for just a scrap of edible food.

Besides the constant danger of TV subtly chipping away at my values, there are some other drawbacks:

Hampers Relations. Who wants to sit around talking and relating with the family when they can get wrapped up in a fantastic, action-packed, no-commitment fantasy?

Destroys Time. The average amount of time we watch TV is about 3½ hours per day. That's 24 hours every week and *52 days every year!* Imagine what we could do with that full extra day each week, those 52 extra days each year if we were to invest them in ourselves or in God? That's exactly how David Wilkerson (founder of Teen Challenge and author of *The Cross and the Switchblade*) got started. He set aside all those hours he'd spent in front of the set and began using that time to pray. As a result his life (and our world) has never been the same.

Requires Little Intellect. The general rule of thumb for TV writers is to write for someone at junior high level. "Don't challenge the audience," they say. "Don't make them think." In fact, sitcoms are often referred to in the business simply as "mind candy."

Distorts Reality. Real life becomes a bore. I mean, what can compare to the fast-paced, special-effect, music-filled action-adventures? Or the hot 'n' steamy passions that are supposed to be real love? (I wonder how many divorces are happening because couples think love is supposed to be like what they see on the screen.) Also, it can create unrealistic expectations of ourselves that may lead to depression and even self-hatred.

Now it's true: TV can educate, it can entertain, and it has the potential for much good. All I'm suggesting is that you be careful. Make sure you're the one using it—don't let it use you.

Motion Pictures

As someone who is directly involved in the film industry, I know how important it is to carefully evaluate movies and videos. I try to be smart in selecting which I will watch. I ask around. I check out the posters, the ads. Do they contain scenes I don't want roaming around inside my mind? Do they touch on a certain weakness I know the Lord is working on?

Violence and profanity have never been a temptation for me. And if necessary for my job I might see a movie or video with those characteristics. But since sensuality has always been a battle inside my head, I won't even go near a "PG" if I know it has sexy situations.

Again, just be smart. You've only got one mind. Don't let anyone dirty it up.

All this to say . . .

Whether we like it or not, the media has a powerful effect on our lives—on what we think, what we feel, what we believe. And whether we like it or not, the old adage is true: We really are what we eat.

If we fill our minds with garbage, rest assured, that's what we'll become. But if we do a little work to find out what's good, and digest that, then that's what we can become.

Once again the decision is ours . . .

Finally, brothers, whatever is true, whatever is noble, whatever is right, whatever is pure, whatever is lovely, whatever is admirable—if anything is excellent or praiseworthy —think about such things (Philippians 4:8).

Bill Myers is a screenwriter and film director. This chapter is reprinted from *Hot Topics, Tough Questions,* by Bill Myers. Published by Victor Books, 1987, Scripture Press Publications, Inc., Wheaton, Ill.

Chapter 2

Pornography: Telephone, Magazines, Films, Videos

by Bob Maddux

Background Scripture: Ephesians 5:3-7; 1 Thessalonians 4:3-8

SEVERAL YEARS AGO, America went through a sexual revolution. Restraint was thrown out the window; casual sin was in. Then, with the advent of herpes and AIDS some have noted a decline in promiscuous sexual relationships.

The risks seemed too great. A one-night stand could lead to a life-threatening disease.

Yet with this turnaround in sexual activity, there is one area of perversion that is not declining; rather it is growing. Sexual fantasy is big business. Imaginative sex is considered safe and easy. One well-known porn peddler explained in an article in *Rolling Stone* magazine this assessment of his business:

> The future is assembly line sex, not actual (sex act) . . . but fantasy.[1]

One example of this is telephone sex.

Telephone Sex

Magazines and newspapers advertise sex over the phone to a growing number of customers. In these ads, beautiful models express their desire to make love over the phone. Some companies even sell gift certificates. The service isn't cheap. One phone call can run $35.00 or more. Yet there are millions of people out there willing to pay for it. One commentator suggested that the reason some people prefer to talk out their fantasy rather than go to a prostitute is that they actually believe they are having sex.[2]

A major San Francisco pornographer explained that as long as the caller believes he's having sex, physical contact with the other party isn't that important. In fact, the sexual experience might even be better because the caller can picture the perfect partner, face, and body. It's quite possible that those who indulge in this activity think they're not really doing anything evil or perverse, but rather just safely escaping from their humdrum life for a little mental adventure.

It's just such delusions that make the whole arena of sexual fantasy so dangerous. Unless our society determines to redeem their minds from undisciplined selfishness, the seeds of destruction being sown now will spring up into a harvest of destruction later.

History of the Porno Plague

Sexual perversion and pornography have been with humanity for ages. I saw the evidence of this one summer while in the ancient city of Ephesus. As our guide led us through the ruins of this fascinating city where the apostle Paul witnessed such great revival, he pointed out a strange carving etched in the stone beneath our feet. There in clear sight was an advertisement for a brothel. A woman's face and a foot pointed the way to a place of sex-for-hire. Today, purveyors of illicit sex no longer chisel their promotions in stone, yet the offer still stands; sex can be purchased. And for many, pornography makes it cheap and easy.

America was having problems with illicit material as far back as 1842, when the first federal restrictions were made against the importing of obscene pictures. Our nation's moral standards had changed radically by the middle of the 20th century. In 1957, a district court decided that for something to be obscene it must be determined by this standard:

> Whether to the average person, applying contemporary community standards, the dominant theme of the material taken as a whole appeals to prurient [unwholesome] interest.[3]

Later, in 1966, the definition of obscenity was restricted to include material "utterly without redeeming social value."[4] With such liberal interpretation the floodgates were opened to the pornographers.

Back in 1953, though, pornography had begun to take on new sophistication. Up until the publication of the first *Playboy* magazine, most pornography had been cheaply produced, poorly packaged, and hard to get.

Playboy's first issue featured nude photos of Marilyn

Monroe. *Playboy* had arrived. Its growth was phenomenal. Its first year's circulation went from 70,000 to 175,000.[5]

Twenty years later, the magazine was selling 20 million copies a month. Soon others jumped on the bandwagon and pushed the number of pornographic magazines being published to about 400 million. It wasn't long, however, before more than nudity appeared on the pages of these magazines. By the mid-'60s, group sex and sex with animals found their way into print. Today, even sex with children, some as young as six months old, is illegally displayed in some types of perverted magazines.

Films and Video Porn

Once relegated to under-the-counter marketing, the porn industry is now breaking into every available channel used to reach the American consumer. Some of the new methods for distributing smut are potentially far more dangerous than the "dirty magazine" approach.

We now use modern technology to bring sexual perversion to the theaters and living rooms of America through the graphic method of live-action films and video.

For years, sex shops have shown short, sexually explicit filmstrips. But more recently erotic films have upgraded and expanded their appeal to a more sophisticated audience. One TV newsmagazine reports that pornographic film producers will make 1,700 new porn movies in a year, while the "legitimate" Hollywood film industry will only turn out about 170 new movies.[6]

Presently there are about 700 "adult" theaters in the United States. It is estimated that the patronage at these film houses will run as high as 2 million each year, resulting in $500 million income for the theater owners. Producers who spend $120,000 on a typical feature-length film can expect to double their investments.[7]

What has fueled the continued growth of this type of product in theaters across the nation? It appears that a growing number of our countrymen are not willing merely to dream about perversion but want graphic depiction to inspire their perverted thought life.

One wonders what effect this has on marriages and relationships between sexes in our culture. At a time when our culture is facing a growing struggle with lasting relationships, the fantasies of film sex are working to make the true intimacy God intended to function within marriage a potential victim. Communication and tenderness are thrown out the door while viewers are content to get their stimulation watching others perform sexually.

With the advent of the videocassette recorder (VCR), a whole new realm of potential sexual fantasy has been made available to the American public. To quote a New York pornographic magazine publisher, the potential is enormous:

> Each VCR is a potential vehicle to become a pornographic theater. This makes even the smallest town available for pornography, thus multiplying pornographic theaters a thousand-fold.[8]

A *Newsweek* magazine poll gave these shocking statistics: 40 percent of all VCR owners have bought or rented X-rated videocassettes. (The rating is now, officially, NC-17. But most porn producers do not bother to have their films rated. They automatically slap an X rating on it themselves.) A market that five years ago provided a porn producer with 5 percent of his profit now brings in 70 percent of his revenues.[9]

What possible effect will this present boom in the sale and rental of X-rated videocassettes have on the lives of Americans? Millions of people who would never venture into a sleazy film house can now bring the same graphic material home to view without the embarrassment of being seen in the wrong place or having to endure the company of people who frequent such places. With easy access to such grossly immoral fare, the potential for several things is evident.

First, the appetite for such perversions will only be increased and with it the desensitizing effect that porn has on the natural and biblical approach to sexuality. Second, the potential for such cassettes getting into the hands of children and minors is drastically increased. A person under the legal age is not allowed into an "adult" theater, but youngsters might easily get hold of a parent's cassette while the adults are not home to prevent such a tragedy. The recent change from X rating to NC-17 has brought about an even greater acceptability of pornography. Theaters that would not show an X-rated film, and newspapers that would not advertise one, are featuring those rated NC-17.

Computer Sex

Today, pornographers will use any avenue available to spread their perverted ideas. One method they loudly herald as unstoppable by their religious opponents is that of modern computer technology. A new computer service known as Sextex makes it possible for its customers to communicate by home computer with X-rated stars, review ads for sexual paraphernalia, and talk to other Sextex users "in an uninhibited, uncensored atmosphere for immediate gratification."[10]

Knowing that technically skilled teenage computer fans have used these skills to get into even top-secret government files, the potential for this form of porn being abused by the young is enormous. When one realizes that almost every form of communication is being tapped by perverted sex salesmen, it's enough to make you shudder at the amount of evil being carried electronically all around us (not to mention the longstanding problem of erotic cable TV programs being pumped into American living rooms). What many parents fail to realize is that as they are becoming desensitized to perverted sex, so are their children.

The Effects of Pornography

Perhaps the first problem with pornography is the way it fuels the fantasies of those exposed to it. One thing is certain, people fantasize often. One university study showed that most people experience 7 or 8 fantasies a day, and some have as many as 40 per day.[11]

But what kind of fantasies are people having? Researchers have discovered the most common fantasy among heterosexuals is having sex with someone besides their partner. Yet strangely, homosexual fantasies were listed fourth and fifth among heterosexuals.

Fantasies involving forced sexual encounters were in the top two on the list of women's fantasies, and 25 percent of all fantasies that most people experience included sadomasochism (finding sexual pleasure in giving or receiving physical pain), group sex, and homosexuality.[12]

With all this unnatural mental imagining going on, the question comes up—where do these thoughts come from? Pornography has long been a recognized source for sexual fantasy. Some sexual therapists even go so far as to encourage couples to view sexually explicit material to enhance their sex lives.[13] Yet, what is the effect on communication, openness, and genuine lovemaking when married partners aren't thinking about one another but about some other "dream lover"?

Many caught up in fantasies actually prefer fantasy to reality. It's easier to control and mold unreal images and daydreams. But when these daydreams begin to spill over into reality, the problems tend to multiply. Studies have shown that pornography can lead to sexual deviance even in normal people.

An organization known as the Free Congress Foundation reported that porn is used by the majority of violent sex offenders.[14] Research has concluded that even brief exposure to filmed scenes of rape can propel the viewer toward antisocial behavior. It can also reinforce the concept that women want to be raped.[15]

The FBI, in a special study, interviewed 36 convicted sex killers. From their research they discovered some startling facts: The killers have had long-standing fantasies that were just as real to them as the acts themselves; the killers' biggest sexual focus was reading sexually explicit materials; the majority of the perpetrators eventually attempted to act out their fantasies on their victims. The tendency to get bored at a certain level and then go on to the more bizarre was also the case, stated one of the killers.[16]

It can be argued that the large majority of pornography readers will not be violent sex offenders. Yet pornography's power most certainly will have some kind of negative effect on a normal, healthy individual. With foreign issues of *Playboy* introducing girls as young as 16 to its pages, those who view such display of adolescent nudity will be tempted more than ever to accept sex with minors as normal behavior in our society.[17]

Researcher Judith Reisman showed that *Penthouse, Playboy,* and *Hustler* magazines contain cartoons depicting children having sex with older people.[18] Gradually, our society is being pushed to the limits of perversion. Magazines like those mentioned can be found in convenience stores and often are within easy reach of minors.

With famous TV stars and athletes posing for nude photo sessions, we have been asked to accept such behavior as a sophisticated and normal part of our culture. Women who display themselves for such pictures are hurting not only themselves but also those who love them. In an interview, the boyfriend of a *Playboy* centerfold told of the rage he felt toward photographers who took the pictures, as well as his embarrassment knowing his friends, along with millions of other men, would be lustfully looking at her naked body.[19]

Pornographers are pushing the outer limits of perversion. Women bound and chained being whipped for the pleasure of the viewer can be seen in sex shop peep shows across the country. In one film, a man pays a prostitute to call him "Dogface" and beat him until he puts on a dog chain, barks like a dog, and eats from a dog dish.[20]

One thing is clear, whether it be hard-core or soft-core, pornography is having its effect on our society. If fantasies can be bought for the right price, then perhaps soon the realities we have considered normal for decades will be pushed aside to be replaced by displays of perversion to feed the appetites of those who have the money to pay for such decadence. Fantasies like these should never become reality, yet the evidence shows that sadly this is not the case.

---

1. Lynn Hirshberg, "Giving Good Phone," *Rolling Stone Yearbook 1983,* 141.

2. Ibid.

3. "The Porno Plague," *Time* (April 5, 1976), 58.

4. Ibid.

5. Peter Bogdonovitch, *The Killing of the Unicorn* (New York: Morrow, 1984), 15-16.

6. *National Federation of Decency Journal* (October 1985), 16.

7. "This Isn't Shakespeare," *Newsweek* (March 18, 1985), 62.

8. Martin Mawyer, *Moral Majority Report* (August 1985), 3.

9. *Newsweek,* March 18, 1985, 61.

10. Mawyer, *Moral Majority Report.*

11. Daniel Goleman, "Sex Fantasies," *Sacramento Bee* (March 8, 1984), 3.

12. Ibid.

13. "The Porno Plague," *Time* (April 5, 1976), 62.

14. Christian Update, *Christian Herald* (July/August 1985), 4.

15. "Sexual Violence in the Media," *Psychology Today* (January 1984), 14.

16. "Deadly Fantasies Spurred Killers, FBI Study Says," *Tacoma New Tribune,* September 26, 1985, 2.

17. *National Federation of Decency Journal,* 11.

18. Ibid., 8.

19. Bob Greene, "Girlfriend Shed It All," *Sacramento Bee* (March 21, 1984), AA2.

20. Mawyer, *Moral Majority Report,* 4.

Bob Maddux is an ordained minister and president of Ridgecrest Academy of Arts in San Ramon, Calif. This chapter is reprinted from *Fantasy Explosion,* by Bob Maddux. © 1986, Regal Books, Ventura CA 93006. Used by permission.

Chapter 3

Contemporary Music: Rock, Pop, and Country

by Bob Maddux

Background Scripture: Psalm 57:7-11; Ezekiel 11:9-12; 2 Corinthians 3:18

THE RHYTHM of the music pounds into the audience like a pile driver. The air is heavy with the smell of sweaty bodies. Thousands of people in the audience are on their feet, many with hands in the air, shouting out the lyrics along with the singers on stage.

Suddenly, just as the music reaches the right decibel, a girl clad in a G-string and tied to a torture rack has a black hood put over her head. Then one of the band members pretends to beat her on the head. Fake blood flows over her body as he attacks her.[1]

Is this a scene from an X-rated movie? No, it's a concert by one of the heavy-metal rock groups around today.

In a separate concert, when the rock star walks on stage, near-worshipful clapping and shouting fill the large exhibition hall. He is clad in the most outrageous clothing his costume designers can create. A female member of his group, naked from the waist up, slithers onto the stage. Reaching down, she pulls a supposed fan from the audience onto the stage, and then in front of everyone begins simulated lovemaking. As the concert continues, the musical lyrics graphically describe a vivid array of sexual activities.[2]

If these concerts were not enough to cause us concern, what about the ongoing assault that pours forth from millions of stereos, AM/FM radios, and clothing store sound systems. We hardly have a quiet moment for reflection.

All of this would not be nearly as dangerous if it weren't for the fact that much of what's being portrayed through secular music today is immoral and selfish, if not totally depraved. Parents who were shocked years ago with the wild antics of Elvis Presley or the Beatles would be totally devastated if they took the time to listen to one of their teenager's records. Susan Baker, wife of the secretary of state, made this observation:

> Some of these lyrics reinforce all the wrong kinds of values for children at a very tender age. For many adults, the beat of such songs is so heavy and the words so indistinguishable that it takes a while to catch on. One of my friends had been exercising to this music for hours before she became aware of the lyrics.[3]

Certainly not all secular music can be classified in the same category, but the trend is one of frightening sensuality and godless philosophy.

The Lyrics

A Russian Communist leader once said that with 26 little soldiers (the letters of the alphabet), he could conquer the world. He understood the power of the written word. Yet in the closing years of the 20th century, there appears to be an even more powerful force for conquering lives, that is, the spoken word linked with the magic of contemporary music.

Anyone who finds themselves in the middle of their morning shower singing the lyrics to a fast-food restaurant's jingle knows the power music has to make words stick in our minds. After a while it can be annoying if not a bit humorous. It can also mean big bucks for the hamburger chain whose name is remembered. The problem with the "jingles" of most secular music is that they're not selling hamburgers.

The lyrics of many of today's minstrels have stepped over the line of decency, and their message has become laced with graphic descriptions of sexual activity.

A few years ago, Capitol Hill was ablaze in a controversy over the lyrics. The wives of top government officials were upset. In their concern, they were trying to bring the record industry and artists to task over the apparent spread of illicit and pornographic lyrics on many of today's popular record albums. The wives paraded by a congressional committee a display of sexually explicit songs, whose lyrics make even grown-ups blush. These words have become common knowledge to millions of teens.

The now tame lyrics of Mick Jagger singing "Let's Spend the Night Together" have given way to the likes of "Sugar Walls," a song clearly reveling in genital arousal. And songs like "Darling Nikki" by Prince have left little to the imagination with lyrics that talk about a girl named Nikki, a sex fiend he meets in a hotel lobby; she is masturbating while looking at a magazine.[4]

Some might suggest these songs are only samples of fringe artists, yet no one will deny the popularity of Madonna, who, on her triple platinum album *Like a Virgin,* sang "Feels So Good Inside."

Only recently have we seen musicians being called into question for their lyrics. In October 1990, 2 Live Crew was acquitted of obscenity charges for "rapping" crudely explicit lyrics that dwelled on oral and anal sex. The 45-minute show was for "adults only." But a record store owner was convicted on an obscenity charge for selling the Crew's "As Nasty as They Wanna Be" recording.

Heavy Metal

Heavy-metal groups take their listeners even farther out. One group, Judas Priest, sang "Eat Me Alive," the words depicting a girl being forced at gunpoint to commit oral sex. Even more explicit are the words of songs by groups like W.A.S.P. For example, the lyrics of one of their songs speaks of naked women lying on the bed and the smell of sweet convulsion and about howling in heat and finally, about committing the sex act, like a beast.[5]

Other unsettling items include blatant occult songs like Grim Reaper's "See You in Hell," a song glorifying satanism.[6]

For some who have heard the message of today's pop music, the words are having an effect. Youth workers, school leaders, and drug abuse counselors sadly report stories of music's power in molding the actions of many of those they deal with.

Country and Western

Rock music is not the only segment of the music industry that is turning out immoral messages through its songs.

Adults would do well to turn a deaf ear to the "middle of the road" singer who croons about adulterous one-night stands, or the country and western tunes that glorify cheating on your mate and rebelling against authority.

Sometimes it's the subtle, smooth sound of a velvet voice that has encouraged a wife struggling in her mind with adulterous fantasies to carry them out.

Performers' Life-styles

Just as influential as the lyrics of their songs are the life-styles of the performers. Rock magazines with full-color pictures glorify the lives of these "rock gods." Their pages are full of vivid accounts of the musical star's living habits.

"My bottle of Jack Daniels is my best friend in the world," boasts Nikki Sixx in one interview.[7] In another, he boldly states, "People think we're wild and crazy all the time. Well, they're right . . . we go through women like most people go through socks."[8]

Newspaper and magazine articles on these "heroes of hedonism" abound, giving the graphic details of the rebellious and depraved actions many of them carry out daily. Trashing hotel rooms, ripping things up, and biting people until their victims are black and blue is just one account reported in one periodical.[9]

A steady diet of idolizing and worshiping these musical stars can create in people's minds the desire to imitate the life-styles of their idols. The fantasy can start out as a playful diversion with young people dressing and talking like their role models. But the lyrics of heavy metal, coupled with the costumes and worldview of the bands, tell kids it's OK to do whatever you want to do: sex, drugs, and rock and roll.

Psychologists have known for years the power of music to change our mental attitudes and emotions. A marketing professor at Loyola University discovered in a study of retail store music that even the background melodies can affect shoppers' moods and increase sales. Restaurants use mood music to increase the patience of waiting customers. Manufacturers have found they can actually "program" their workers for greater efficiency.[10]

If, as the researchers say, positive music can manipulate us positively, then it's also possible that the negative images projected through much secular music can mold the lives of the listeners in a destructive way.

Need for Christian Expression

Against this tide, Christian artists are attempting to raise up a standard through their own religious songs and videos. Some of these work quite well, while others offer only a milder form of what the world puts out. It will take more than "Christian" girls in tight pants dancing to the lead singer's surly singing to draw the world to the Lord. Let us pray that in attempting to reach the world, these artists don't copy the world so much that the message is buried in the same sensuous fantasy we're trying to lead them away from.

I warmly applaud any sincere, Spirit-guided attempt to be creative in this area. I believe the door for positive Christian expression through this medium is wide open. The God who is called Creator can certainly give us the kind of creativity to command the attention even of a world jaded by the lifeless themes of violence, sex, drugs, and the occult.

---

1. Kandy Strand, "My Turn," *Newsweek* (May 6, 1985).

2. Reported by a youth pastor who attended the concert as a concerned observer.

3. David Gergen, "K-Rated Records," *U.S. News and World Report* (May 20, 1985), 98.

4. "Parents vs. Rock," *People* (September 16, 1985), 46-51.

5. "Rock Is a Four-Letter Word," *Time* (September 30, 1985), 70.

6. "See You in Hell" (© Eboy Ltd., 1983, 1984).

7. "Motley Crue Speak Out," *Hit Parader* (March 1985), 54.

8. Ibid., 52.

9. "White Noise, How Heavy Metal Rules," *Village Voice* (June 18, 1985), 48.

10. "How Muzak Manipulates You," *Science Digest* (May 1984).

Bob Maddux is an ordained minister and president of Ridgecrest Academy of Arts in San Ramon, Calif. This chapter is reprinted from *Fantasy Explosion*, by Bob Maddux, © 1986, Regal Books, Ventura, CA 93006. Used by permission.

Chapter 4

The Sanctification of Sport

by Shirl J. Hoffman

Background Scripture: Zechariah 8:5; 1 Corinthians 10:31; Colossians 3:12-14

ASK good Presbyterians the old catechism question, "What is the chief end of man?" and they likely will respond, "To glorify God and enjoy Him forever."

Likewise, ask evangelical athletes, "Why do you play sports?" and there is a good chance they will echo the words of former Pittsburgh Pirate Manny Sanguillen: "I just want to glorify God, that's why I play ball."

Humorist Roy Blount, Jr., claims that so many Christians have invaded big-time football that, when he set out to select an "All-Religious Team" and an "All-Heathen Team," he couldn't find enough heathens to field a squad.

There is a trend toward mixing sport and religion. But I am not optimistic that it will stimulate a much-needed rethinking of the meaning of sport among the evangelical community in general.

Competition as Worship?

The chances that that will happen are not good, for one critical reason: In presuming to play "to the glory of God," the Christian athletes confront an inevitable contradiction.

Sport, which celebrates the myth of success, is harnessed to a theology that often stresses the importance of losing.

Sport, which symbolizes the morality of self-reliance and teaches the just rewards of hard work, is used to propagate a theology dominated by the radicalism of grace ("The first shall be the last, and the last first").

In addition, church tradition and the Scriptures quite clearly teach the importance of purity in the actions offered as rituals of worship. The New Testament Christians were just as concerned about the acceptability of their symbolic offerings as the Old Testament priests and prophets were about the purity of their animal sacrifices. Christians would not think of consecrating acts of robbery or murder as worship. Nor would they condone worshipers enacting the liturgy while harboring feelings of jealousy, hate, or a thirst for revenge.

Yet anyone close to the sports scene knows that competition, even between the most amiable opponents, often becomes a rite of unholy unction, a sacrament in which aggression is vented, old scores settled, number one taken care of, and where the discourteous act looms as the principal liturgical gesture. Even in contests played in the shadow of church walls—the church league softball or basketball game—tempers can flare, and the spiritual graces of compassion and sensitivity can place second to "winning one for good ol' First Baptist."

The psychological dimension of competition has always been a touchy subject among Christians, most of whom downplay its importance in the competitive process. And they do so for good reason. Any objective appraisal of the competitive process will reveal that it is driven by the spirit of self-promotion.

Self-promotion is the lifeblood of competitive games. Those who would give the game an honest try (and this is widely held to be a spiritual duty of the Christian athlete) must make a sincere effort to win. And within the context of the game, "trying to win" means promoting one's own (or the team's) interest at the expense of the opponent's interest.

In a spirited but frank defense of competition, sailor Stuart Walker avowed that good competitors should "feel no concern for the opinion and feelings of others." The lack of concern for the feelings of competitors is useful because it eliminates a distraction. If you don't care what the other fellow thinks, Walker said, you can cut in on him wherever you wish.

The Christian Killer Instinct

There is common sense in Walker's philosophy. Consider a sympathetic tennis player who is constantly worried about the detrimental effects of her serve on her opponent's performance. Let's say that in a gesture of sympathy and goodwill, she decreases the ball's velocity and spin, and places it conveniently in the center of the service area. Not only would she win few championships, she would be ridiculed (even by her opponent) as a dangerous subversive, a spoilsport who violated the unwritten contract by not giving the game an honest try.

Just as surely as sympathetic instincts can douse the fires of competition, a cool, calculated insensitivity toward opponents can fan them into a blaze. The so-called killer instinct is widely believed to be indispensable for athletic success.

In an analysis of winning and losing attitudes among athletes, sport psychologist Bruce Ogilvie reported: "Almost every truly great athlete we have interviewed during the last four years . . . has consistently emphasized that in order to be a winner you must retain the killer instinct."

How much better feelings of sympathy can be controlled if opponents are viewed as dangerous enemies. Jimmy Connors' meteoric rise to the top in professional tennis was accompanied by a brash demeanor that shocked the staid tennis aristocracy. He berated officials, made obscene gestures, and openly chided his opponents. Said Connors: "Maybe my methods aren't socially acceptable to some, but it's what I have to do to survive. I don't go out there to love my enemy, I go out there to squash him."

Even coaching legend Vince Lombardi saw the need to conjure up "competitive animosity" toward the opponent during the week before the big game. This belief was captured in his oft-quoted remark, "To play this game, you must have that fire in you, and nothing stokes that fire like hate."

There is clinical evidence to show that Vince was not just talking through his helmet. In a study of differences between habitually successful and unsuccessful competitors, Francis Ryan, former psychologist and track coach at Yale, discovered that good competitors viewed their opponents as temporary enemies. But poor competitors, "rather than whipping up their anger to meet the competitive challenge, did everything possible to maintain an atmosphere of friendliness with their opponents."

Locker-room Religion

Athletes have not found it easy to combine Christian spirituality and winning competitiveness. Asked how he blended football with faith, former Cincinnati Bengal Ron Pritchard said, "I'm probably not at the point where I can turn the other cheek all the time. I'd like to be able to say, 'Hey, God loves you and I love you, and I'll see you later.' But I'm not there yet; but with God's help, I'll make it someday."

Doug Plank, formerly a hard-hitting defensive back for the Chicago Bears, called his athletic and religious life a paradox: "As a Christian I learn to love, but when the whistle blows I have to be tough. You're always walking a tightrope." The trick to walking the tightrope (which few seem to have mastered) is to temper competitive enthusiasm with just the right amount of spiritual grace, igniting the necessary competitive fire without marring one's Christian witness.

This is the plight of evangelical athletes. They want very much to see their performances as acts of worship. Yet they are not entirely sure that sport is worthy of sacred offering.

In a desperate attempt to harmonize these clashing elements of ritual, evangelicals have concocted a locker-room religion. It is not so much orthodox Christianity as a hodgepodge of biblical truths, worn-out coaching slogans, Old Testament allusions to religious wars, and interpretations of Paul's metaphors that would drive the most straight-laced theologian to drink.

The most popular doctrine in this locker-room religion is "Total Release Performance," promulgated throughout the evangelical network by an organization called Champions for Excellence. "The quality of an athlete's performance can reveal the quality of his love for God," says that organization's president, Wes Neal. The quality most valued is intensity, the same kind of intensity Jesus had—

"His total concentration toward accomplishing His Father's purpose."

Total Release Performance (initiates refer to it simply as TRP) has become a familiar watchword for evangelical athletes, a ritual for identifying the faithful. Shouted across lines of scrimmage or whispered in the huddle, TRP is a cosmic energizer, the athletic equivalent of the Pentecostal's "Praise the Lord" or the Nazarene's "Amen."

So forcefully has the doctrine behind the motto shaped the beliefs of Christian athletes, they rarely talk about sport as worship without mentioning the critical contingency of total release. Pro footballer Archie Griffin painted crosses on his shoes and wristbands as a reminder that he was playing to glorify Christ and not himself. "All you can ask of yourself is that you give 110 percent. I want to please Christ, and I can't be happy if I'm giving any less than that," Griffin said.

Belting another person around on a football field may seem an odd way to express your love to him or to the Almighty. But in what may be the most puzzling theological conundrum to come out of the movement, former Los Angeles Ram Rich Saul once warned his Christian opponents, "I'm going to hit you guys with all the love I have in me."

Grahams of the Gridiron

Another way evangelicals have sought to sanctify competitive sport has been to concentrate on the evangelistic potential of sport. In a society that lauds competitive success, winning in athletics offers a visible platform from which athletes can publicly declare their witness.

Record-setting Walter Payton of the Chicago Bears says, "I realized in my second year that for me, performing well on the field and doing well as a professional football player made little kids look up to me. God enabled me to communicate with them. I found out that this was the way Christ wanted me to spread His message. My professional performance is God's way of using me to reach out and touch kids and bring them to Christ."

Turning in stellar individual performances, Payton certainly increased his evangelistic potential. It was raised even higher when the Bears put together a Super Bowl season. As Roger Staubach, reflecting on the Cowboys' win over Miami in the 1972 Super Bowl, said: "I had promised that it would be for God's honor and glory, whether we won or lost. Of course the glory was better for God and me since we won, because the victory gave me a greater platform from which to speak."

But by using sport as a net to catch sinners' souls, the evangelicals worsen the nagging conflicts. When sport is harnessed to the evangelistic enterprise, evangelicals become as much endorsers of the myths reinforced by popular sport ("winning is everything") as they do of the Christian gospel.

A New Sports Ethic

There is a way out for evangelicals, a way they can more closely align their athletic rituals to the devotion and beliefs they wish to express. There is a way to cancel (or at least lessen) contradictions between faith and action, a way to insure that the seeds of the movement will lead to a reconceptualization of the meaning of sport in the Christian life. This would require Christians to build a new sports ethic from the ground up.

Here are a few thoughts—a start, perhaps—about what a Christian sports ethic might look like.

First, we should recognize that against the backdrop of the current sport ethic, a Christian ethic is likely to be viewed as irrational. Don't expect a Christian ethic to fit snugly inside the reigning secular ethic.

Second, recognize that there is nothing like one's play life to make one transparent. Plato once said you can learn a lot more about a person in an hour of play than in a year of conversation. Be prepared to deal with those character flaws that are brought to the surface during the excitement of the contest. Do not dismiss them as part of the game; they are the true person.

Third, recognize that if sport is to be sport at all, the objective of winning must *not* be de-emphasized. The prospect of winning lies at the very heart of competitive sport. Contests in which the prospects of winning have been forfeited are heartless, pointless encounters that lack purpose and incentive for the participants.

The spoilsport who does not try to win is worse than a cheat. The cheat robs the game of its noble spirit; but the spoilsport steals its very heart.

At the same time, however, we must be careful not to delude ourselves into thinking that God in any way cares about the outcome. Those who feel that God especially cherishes winners—or that a win somehow glorifies Him more than a loss—have theologically reduced God to a spectator who sits on the sidelines caught up in the surprises of the contest.

Finally, although the objective of the contest is to win, the reason for participating far surpasses a concern for the actual outcome. Christians should play for one reason: to celebrate a joyous life, secure in Christ. Sports for the Christian should reflect none of the tension, aggravation, and maliciousness evident in secular sport.

More than in any other aspect of his life, the play life of the Christian should be lighthearted; it should be a festive time in which the quality of play is enhanced simply because the game is a tribute to our Heavenly Father.

Perhaps we should seize hold of Zechariah 8:5 as a standard we might use to judge our play. Zechariah 8:5 presents a vision of the coming age, a vision in which the streets of the city are full of boys and girls playing. Playing is but a feeble imitation of what is in store for us in the blessed world to come. Think of it! Our play life can be an imitation of our life for all eternity. Would we be happy with our sport for eternity, or should we begin changing it?

Shirl J. Hoffman is professor and chair of the Department of Physical Education at the University of North Carolina, Greensboro.

Chapter 5

Dressing for Spiritual Success

by Rick Bundschuh

Background Scripture: Matthew 6:19-21; Luke 12:15-21; 1 Timothy 2:9; 1 Peter 3:3-4

BLUE JEANS. The all-American garment. What could be a more appropriate choice for both sexes to wear if they were going to be involved in a grubby workday at a Mexican orphanage just the other side of the border?

Under the early morning overcast a score of high school students crawled into cars and vans to make the trip across the border. They were young, devout, and innocent. They had given up their Saturday to help those who could not help themselves. As they jostled their blue-jean-clad knees together over the bumpy roads, they had no idea of the shock in store for them.

As the first vehicle pulled up to the orphanage door, the students poured out of their seats, glad to stretch after the long ride. At the same time the kids of the orphanage came exploding out of the building to check out the visitors and be first in line for any "blessings" in the form of fruit or candy they might have brought with them.

One of the blue-jeaned girls approached a young boy of about 10 with a large, brilliantly orange tangerine. "¿Tu quieres?" (Would you like some?) she asked in her best high school Spanish. The crowd of children giggled, whispered, and occasionally pointed at the American girls in their clean Levi's.

One of the guys in the group, Chuey, was bilingual. Raised in a Puerto Rican home, he found Spanish as natural as English. He engaged the orphans in discussion immediately. It was small talk about spitting tangerine seeds and eating lemons whole. It was he who first overheard the word in a whisper. "Prostitutes," whispered one of the older orphans to another.

"What did you say?" asked Chuey in Spanish. The boy turned red and tried to hide his face down in his coat. "Where?" asked Chuey. The kid hesitated for a few moments and then jabbed a pointed finger quickly toward the girl passing out fruit from the back of a van. "Prostitute?" inquired Chuey in Spanish. "Why do you think that?"

"Pants," replied the boy. "They are all wearing pants, and everyone knows that only prostitutes wear pants."

Chuey was shocked and taken aback at the obvious cultural valley he had just fallen into. He tried to explain that in the United States most girls wear pants at least some of the time. He was not sure that his explanation was being received. These kids had never been north of the border. All they knew of what life was like was what they had seen in the little *colonia* or colony in which they lived. Chuey even noticed the neighbors standing in the doorways and pointing. He could imagine them saying to one another, "What are all those prostitutes doing at the orphanage?"

Chuey went to the leader of the group with the revelation. The leader was surprised and then quiet for a moment. Then he asked all the girls wearing pants to climb into the cars. For them, the workday was already over, but their horror was just beginning as they were told that they had been mistaken for benevolent hookers. They waited on the other side of the border for their male counterparts to finish working.

The next workday planned by the group was accompanied by a large announcement that said, "All Girls Must Wear Dresses."

This incident may strike you as humorous, unfair, sexist, petty, ignorant, or just silly. Regardless of how you feel about blue jeans being the attire of prostitutes, it is clear that clothing styles communicate different things to different people.

Clothing in Bible Times

The first recorded clothing was a quickly assembled array of fig leaves, cheap but tough to put through the washing machine. The clothes of most of the people in the Bible consisted of a square-cut cloth of linen or wool. The basic costume was unisex, but the differences between men's and women's clothing were evident in designs and decorations woven into the ladies' robes. Clothes made of rare materials such as silk were considered the prized possessions of the wealthy. Most people had few if any changes of garment.

The status of a person was often indicated by the kind of clothes he was privileged to wear.

The Bible does not make a big deal out of clothes. It warns us that members of one sex should not go around dressed like the other sex (see Deuteronomy 22:5). Scripture also warns us not to put all of our energy into dressing up the outside but rather to put our energy into adorning the inside (see 1 Peter 3:3-4).

Even though the Bible is relatively quiet about clothing, many Christians are not. In some churches the pulpit rings with condemnation of various types of fashion and hairstyles. Christian homes often erupt into full-blown wars over hair, makeup, or clothing. If the Bible is so quiet, why do Christians make so much noise? The answer is not always an easy one, but it may have to do with some of the following observations.

Clothing Communicates

For most Western people, clothes have far more than a practical function of warmth and protection. They are a costume. They are a uniform. They say what role you are playing, what side you are on, or what ideas you subscribe to. Even bizarre-looking people tend to look similarly bizarre. Some say they are trying to be different, but how come all the different people look so oddly similar? Why is it someone who wants to be different isn't really different?

In the selection of our costume we make subtle or obvious statements. We identify ourselves to one degree or another.

Some kids in the early 1960s loved to wear replicas of iron crosses around their necks. Most of them didn't have a reason for doing it other than it drove their folks crazy to see their offspring wearing the symbol of a nation they fought against in World War II. The crazier it drove the parents, the more cool it was to wear the dumb things. The main reason that most kids wore the crosses was that other kids did it and it showed they were really independent of their parents' values—even if they were good values.

Clothing is more costume than covering in Western cultures. Because of this, if a person sees the values and ideas of something evil (such as Nazi fascism) being represented by the costume of another (especially if that person is a member of the same household or church), it is no wonder there is a loud outcry of protest.

Of course the difficulty with labeling a costume is that some of the darkest and most evil people in the world wear nice suits and look conservatively clean-cut. If we were to label a costume selfish, greedy, or merciless, what would it look like?

Some people wear costumes that are designed to stimulate others sexually or to heighten the wearer's sensuality. Some wear such clothing in ignorance, others wear it with intent. The result is usually the same: It attracts the opposite sex for the wrong reason. In some ways this is much like the old trick of taping a "Kick Me" sign to some poor sucker's back and then watching the person get booted down the hall. Except those who dress to be sexy often place the "Kick Me" (or "Use Me") signs on their own backs. Their costume is the surface evidence of a much deeper problem that needs to be dealt with by God's love and compassion.

Some people wear clothing to show off their economic status and all-around good taste. They generally spend most of their time impressing each other, since the average toad on the street doesn't give a rip if a coat costs $1,000 or $20.00. Again, these people are almost to be pitied rather than scorned, since their lives are so bankrupt of character they must get their worth out of at least looking successful.

Clothing Costs Money

There is another element that comes into play when a Christian begins to wrestle with the issue of clothing and culture. That element is called stewardship, or the right use of money.

Clothes cost money, sometimes big money. Christians must deal not only with the desire to stay in style culturally but with the fact that each dollar they have is a gift from God to be used wisely and compassionately. This should cause Christians to ask themselves questions that those who do not know Christ seldom ask. "Do I need this pair of shoes badly enough to spend $120 on them?" "Should I sink hundreds of dollars into an outfit I will probably wear only once?" "Should I buy this outrageously styled and colored shirt, knowing full well that it has a short life expectancy for being stylish—and a tall price tag?"

These considerations cover not only clothes but also jewelry, makeup, and anything else that is dangled, draped, or drilled on our body. How much gold and how many jewels a Christian should own and display is too complex a question to dive into in a chapter on clothes, but it is one of those thorny issues that *needs* to be handled by every believer who is seriously investing God's money toward them.

The Moving Line of Modesty

Another fence for Christians in the area of clothes comes from the teaching of Scripture encouraging modesty (see 1 Timothy 2:9). The difficulty is that this fence seems to shift depending on the time and culture we find ourselves in. For instance, we would be outraged if a man showed up for dinner wearing a long wig, makeup, a ruffled blouse, silk pantaloons (tight pants), and stockings. It is completely inappropriate attire. But it was the way true gentlemen such as Mozart, Washington, and Jefferson dressed when going out.

We might think the Christians of a South American jungle tribe immodest for their lack of clothing in the tropical heat; they would think us silly for our abundance of clothing in the same heat.

Great-great-grandma would have raced to an early grave if she could have seen what her descendants would one day consider modest apparel at the beach. In fact, modesty even varies according to the setting within the culture. What one wears to swim in is not considered modest or appropriate if worn to a concert downtown.

So there are still things that are considered immodest for people to wear. Christians must be conscious of this "moving line" of modesty and do their best to stay within it for the place and times they live in.

Avoid Offending

Another margin by which the costuming of a Christian must be hemmed in is this idea that we are to so love our fellow Christians (and people in general) that we do nothing that will interfere with their spiritual well-being (see 1 Corinthians 10:32). This means being sensitive to what genuinely offends people and cripples their walk with God.

This does not mean we are to be particularly worried about wearing things that others do not personally care for. For example, I do not care for polyester clothing. I think it looks dumb and tacky. This is simply my opinion. I am right as long as *I* don't wear polyester clothes. I am wrong once I start telling *you* not to. You would do better to ignore me and let me grow up by figuring out that I cannot and should not impose my personal tastes on you.

With so many conditions and things to think about, it may seem easier just to chuck it and wear whatever you want whenever you want to. It may be easier, but it does not help us grow in our Christian lives. It may be that we really do need to stop and rethink our "costume." Is the message we give really what we want to say? Is the costume worth the hassles in our family relationships? Is the money we spend going toward things that will matter in eternity?

How Important Is Good Looks?

Probably one of the saddest things about clothing and our culture is that for many the exterior, the costume, the hair, the makeup, and the "look" are tremendously important.

It is not wrong to take care of what God has given us and to do the best job we can sprucing up our "earthly temple." Obviously a clean, fresh-smelling person is a much nicer person to be around than someone with the odor of mildew seeping from his clothing. At the same time, we must get our perspective correct. The clothes will rot, the hair will thin, and the body will sag regardless of what we do to try to stop it. Time and gravity play the same brutal tricks on all things made of flesh. If our lives are invested in externals, we are in dire straits. Our energy should first be directed toward the inside, to make us presentable in character. The excess of that energy should then spill over into the cosmetics of life.

Jesus himself said, "A man's life does not consist in the abundance of his possessions" (Luke 12:15). He also asked the rhetorical question, "What can a man give in exchange for his soul?" (Mark 8:37). The answer to that question might very well be: "Money, fashion, style, and the longing to be respected by others." Our Lord also had a stern warning: "Do not store up for yourselves treasures on earth, where moth and rust destroy, and where thieves break in and steal" (Matthew 6:19).

The horrible truth is that for many people—even some who call themselves Christian—their treasure hangs in the closet, rests on shoe racks, and lies sleeping in jewelry boxes. Such treasure gives a false hope, a temporary feeling of being somebody while the somebody we were created to be lies unexplored.

Ultimately it will make little difference to God what we look like on the outside, but it will make an incredible difference to Him what we are like on the inside.

For those struggling or battling with clothes, hair, jewelry, makeup, and the rest of the trappings of our culture, we have the biblical guidelines of modesty, care of the spiritual well-being of others, stewardship of money, and the desire to work on the inner person with greater urgency and care than we work on the outer appearance.

Rick Bundschuh is a youth worker and director of Youth Products at Gospel Light Publications. Reprinted from *Hot Buttons,* by Rick Bundschuh, © 1986, Regal Books, Ventura, Calif. Used by permission.

Chapter 6

The Simple Life
in a Complex World

by Rebecca Laird

Background Scripture: Psalm 24:1; 1 Timothy 6:17-18

THE TRAIN my husband and I rode from Paris arrived at the Macon station after dark. Michael and I disembarked and waited for a bus bound for the tiny village of Taize (TAY-zay). When we found out the bus loaded at a different stop, our hearts sank.

We had traveled for hours to reach the Community of Taize, an ecumenical monastery internationally known for its commitment to reconciliation through prayer and worship. We had to get to Taize that night. Our time in France was limited to a week.

The information desk at the station posted a list of telephone numbers for taxis. As the temperature dropped on the late November night, I called the first number on the list. Relying on my years of college French, I tried to hire a cab.

I hung up and told Michael, "I think we are to wait outside for a silver car with a blonde woman driver." My husband looked at me skeptically. I was relieved when a silver car pulled into the station and the blonde woman asked, "Taize?"

Forty minutes later we turned onto a winding road and stopped just beyond a small village. We paid the fare, using all our francs, since we had not planned on taking a taxi. Then we began the final short trek to the home of 50 monks in a monastery recognized by both the Lutheran church and the Roman Catholic church. Lights gleamed from a yellow farmhouse on top of the hill. Inside, a fire roared and we were greeted warmly. Our letter asking if we could visit the Community of Taize had not arrived. Our presence was unexpected, but it didn't alter the welcome extended to us. We were strangers in a foreign land, but we were ushered in as friends.

Pilgrims visit the monastery each year, to pray, to seek reconciliation with spouses, to search for answers to imposing questions. Michael and I heard about Taize through a branch of the community that meets in San Francisco once a month. We attended many of those services.

Within minutes of our arrival, one of the brothers escorted us to a guest house. Our room was simply furnished—two cots, two woolen blankets, a clothes rod with two hangers, a nightstand, chair, and a wooden bowl with shiny fall apples. Someone had prepared for us. We had everything we needed: a warm place to sleep, a place to hang our coats, and something to stay our hunger after a long journey. My eyes filled with tears of gratitude. We were no longer strangers but friends. The warmth of Christian hospitality reached us.

We quickly freshened up, left our belongings, and walked to the chapel. In an open, candlelit room, worshipers joined the white-robed brothers in prayer. Everyone sat on the floor or knelt on unadorned wooden kneeling benches. Together we sang penetrating, meditative songs of praise. The brothers sang in French, English, Spanish, and Latin— purposefully praising God in many languages to express their shared goal of reconciling all the world's people in God. The simple, reverent service moved us deeply.

The ringing of many bells in the arched gate to Taize woke us early the next morning; there were no alarm clocks in the rooms. All gathered for a short service to thank God for a safe night and to welcome God's presence into our day. Breakfast consisted of hot chocolate served in bowls for dunking the crusty bread from the previous night's meal. With no pots, pans, or utensils to wash, and with everyone helping, meal cleanup took a brief time. Everyone soon separated, migrating to an assigned place of work.

Life at Taize is simple and ordered, to allow community members to concentrate their time and energies on the goals of reconciliation and prayer.

The few days spent at Taize clarified for me the purpose of living a simple life. Simplicity unclutters our lives so we can freely obey the call of God. The brothers of Taize don't worry about what they will wear or what they will eat. Instead of adopting the capitalistic value "More is better," they consciously choose to have only what is essential for a healthy life. They live unencumbered lives of moderation and balance. While most people do not live in monastic communities, the values modeled by the brothers of Taize can be helpful to Christians in evaluating how to live in the world.

Today's culture can entice even the most dedicated Christian to become a glutton for new adventures, and greedy for the best and the biggest consumer products. The good life is too often pictured as a big house, a spacious lawn with a swimming pool, and a several-car garage. What this one-dimensional picture does not show is the time and energy the "good life" requires. Cleaning, decorating, and repairing the big house; cutting, pruning, and watering the spacious lawn; and tuning, waxing, and fixing the luxury cars can demand most of the time God graciously allots to each day.

In my household, I often feel overwhelmed with clutter—the junk mail, the old newspapers, the glass jars to recycle, the baby clothes to launder, the memorabilia from vacations, plays, birthdays—the stuff of a busy life. When the clutter begins to bother me, I know it's time to ask myself the question, what is essential for me to be faithful to the calling of God on my life? Then I find ways to simplify, simplify, simplify.

We're Not Owners, God Is

Scripture teaches, "The earth is the Lord's, and everything in it, the world, and all who live in it" (Psalm 24:1). God owns everything—land, gold, cattle, cars, houses, countries, people. When we discover that God is the Owner and we are simply caretakers, our relationship to money and possessions falls into perspective.

It is God's job to create and provide basic nourishment to all of creation. His continual provision of rain and sun helps trees and plants grow so we can enjoy and use them to meet our basic needs. God certainly cares about meeting our needs, but nowhere does He guarantee to pay sky-high mortgages for opulent houses. Nor does He promise to provide the money for weekly restaurant meals.

I believe that God cares more about the tiny boy I met in Calcutta whose parents left him at one of Mother Teresa's orphanages because they could not feed him than He cares about my desire for a third bedroom. The little boy would die without food. I could live without a third bedroom.

Many essentials basic to life differ markedly from culture to culture. I may need a car to stay employed in Los Angeles, where freeways connect communities. I may not need a car in San Francisco, where homes and jobsites are closer together, and where good public transit is available. For missionaries in Papua New Guinea where roads are scarce, a car could be useless, but a motorcycle equipped for rugged terrain may be vital.

Laws cannot force the equal distribution of wealth. Look at the communist countries as a failed example. Only hearts and pockets open for God's use can share wealth in a way that meets each need.

Our job is to manage what God owns. As stewards we are to use our resources wisely, be content with God's allotment, and share with others.

First Timothy 6:17-18 summarizes what it means to be a good steward: "Command those who are rich in this present world not to be arrogant nor to put their hope in wealth, which is so uncertain, but to put their hope in God, who richly provides us with everything for our enjoyment. Command them to do good, to be rich in good deeds, and to be generous and willing to share."

Sue Bender, in *Plain and Simple: A Woman's Journey to the Amish,* illustrates good stewardship. The author noticed while visiting an Amish family of 10 that after two weeks the family had produced but one small container of garbage. They recycled almost everything. They gave organic matter to the animals or spread it on the compost pile. Bender also noticed that many Amish families never threw away old clothes. Instead, they cut the fabric into quilting pieces to make warm, durable coverlets for winter.

Though my life as a city dweller prohibits me from composting, I can refuse to buy products in nonrecyclable packaging. And I can call the local recycling project to have bins delivered to my house to make sorting and pickup easier.

I don't have time for quilting, but I can buy clothing that is durable and washable so when I clean out my closets and donate items to a local clothing room, some needy people may find something they can use.

Good stewardship begins with making wise choices that consider the future usefulness of God's resources rather than just the gratification of our instant desires.

How to Simplify Your Life

So how do we begin to simplify? Here are some principles to start you on your way.

Simplicity begins within. Simplicity must begin with an inner longing rather than an external rule. Until we honestly want a simpler life, so we can live more faithfully, our efforts toward a simpler existence will become legalisms that bind rather than liberate. Richard Foster writes in *Freedom in Simplicity,* "Simplicity is both a grace and a discipline." Conversion to a simpler life comes as a grace, a gift from God. It takes more than willpower to live a consistently simple life. But with the Lord's help, our efforts at unencumbered living make us better available to receive and respond to God's calling.

Simplicity makes us available, not more holy. Living a more simple life will not in itself heighten our spirituality. Instead, our acts of detachment help cultivate an attitude God can use. We empty ourselves so there is room for God to refill. Excessive self-denial is not a Christian ideal. Shunning material goods without an internal call to let go of worldly possessions will only make us proud of our accomplishment.

Possessions are to be used, not revered. God gives us gifts for our use and health, not for us to idolize. Possessions are not bad—not at all. Owning a lakefront cabin is no sin, but keeping it tightly locked for 50 weeks a year so the decor won't get tattered might be if a friend needs to get away for a few days. On the other hand, the fact that you don't own a cabin doesn't make you holy. Especially when you harbor a begrudging spirit or a sense of false pride.

God doesn't give wealth just for our benefit. E. V. Hill, an energetic black preacher from Los Angeles, said it this way, "God gives it to ya, to get it through ya. He doesn't just have you in mind." The bounty of the earth can meet the needs of all of God's people; distribution and priorities are the problems. When we see a need and have resources to help meet it, God may be blessing us to use the works of our hands to bless another. In a consumer society like ours, goods go to the highest bidder. In God's economy, justice rather than the ability to pay determines how resources are divided.

Detachment is a discipline. Letting go of items regularly can become a ritual of worship that shows our desire to depend on God. Giving away a sweater each time we buy a new one is a good practice. Regularly scheduling a closet cleaning day and ridding our home of all items that haven't been used for the past year might be a place to begin. Everything comes from God, thus we don't need to hoard things we don't use.

Simplicity brings freedom. In *Plain and Simple,* Sue Bender asks, "How could pared-down and daring go together?" But they do. As God's pilgrim people, we are called to be ready to move out into the wilderness or toward the Promised Land just as the Israelites did. Pilgrims can't make house and home top priorities; they must be willing to move quickly, taking only what is necessary for the journey.

For some the call may be literally to travel the globe, spreading the compassion of Jesus. For others the call to live simply may be essential to free up time to offer hospitality to the homeless—strangers in our own land. Our responsibility is to begin to sort through and let go so when God speaks we are free to obey and follow.

Simplicity is a life-style, not an achievement. None of us in this fast-paced culture can choose simplicity in all things. We do what we can, but then we must trust that our faithfulness truly pleases God.

Rebecca Laird is a free-lance writer and editor living in San Francisco.

Chapter 7

Trashed People

by Ann Cubie Rearick

Background Scripture: Genesis 19:1-8; Job 8:5-7;
Galatians 3:26-29

WE ALL TREAT PEOPLE AS TRASH at some time or another. We use them, discard them, and ignore them.

Take Billy, for example. He was a likable 13-year-old when I first met him at the juvenile detention center where I served as the Protestant chaplain. He stayed with us just a few days, but during that time I could see he got along well with everyone—the staff as well as the other teens.

But six months later he was back. This time the social worker told me his story. Billy was just one child in a large family with many problems. The problems included alcohol and illegal drugs.

Billy wasn't the oldest of the children, but for some reason his parents took their frustrations out on him. Actually, it isn't that uncommon for parents to single out a child, for no obvious reason, and treat the child differently. Perhaps Billy looked like a family member the parents hated. To make things worse, when parents treat a child harshly, it is pretty common for the other children in the family to join in.

When tensions ran high, Billy's parents kicked him out of the house. He could get the boot at 2 A.M. as easily as at 2 P.M. Out on the street, this 13-year-old would steal so he could eat, and "hang out" until the police picked him up and brought him to the detention center.

In his home, Billy was trash. He was valuable only as someone to blame for the family problems. He was dispensable, a throwaway, the unwanted person in the family.

Billy had a sadness that hovered about him. All who got close enough could sense the deep hurt within. It's painful at any age when the people we think should love us most love us least. But at age 13, it is devastating.

Billy's case isn't an isolated one. In the latest figures available in the United States, there were 2.2 million cases of child abuse reported, according to the American Humane Association. About 40 percent of these were confirmed. I wonder how many other cases were not reported?

These were children who were physically hurt, placed in dangerous situations through neglect, used for the sexual enjoyment of adults, or emotionally harassed with harsh and unfair words.

As a society, we pay for mistreating our children. Most

of the young people brought into publicly funded detention centers have been abused. Many of the boys have suffered violent physical abuse. Many of the girls have endured sexual abuse.

When I served as their chaplain, I would often watch as a new young person was ushered into our detention center. Sometimes in those moments I would think, We abuse our children and then lock them up when they act out their desperation.

How unlike Jesus we can be. It was He who said, "Let the little children come to me, and do not hinder them, for the kingdom of God belongs to such as these" (Mark 10:14). After Jesus said this, He took the children in His arms, put His hands on them, and blessed them.

Many churches are trying to be the arms of Jesus today. They provide day care, nursery schools, and baby-sitting programs for children who get home from school before their parents get home from work.

We devalue other groups of people too.

When I was in chaplaincy training, I worked in a large county hospital. There I met people whom no one outside the hospital seemed to care about.

John was one of these.

A big man once noted for his physical strength, he now sat helplessly, day after day, in a wheelchair. He had chosen as "his spot" a place in the second floor hallway between two wings of the building. "His spot" was a place people often walked by—busy people on the way to either wing, but people whom he hoped would stop and talk. The conversations were usually limited to "Hi, John, how ya doing?"—without waiting to see how John was actually doing.

As the chaplain assigned to this area, John became part of my parish. We talked. I discovered a lonely man who, before a serious automobile accident, had been a vital part of his sister's family. Never married, he had lived with his sister and had given her a portion of his earnings from driving an 18-wheeler. This was to help with the household expenses.

But now, after wrecking his rig and suffering serious head injuries, he was penniless and a permanent resident of a county hospital. He rarely had a visitor.

One day he said, "Chaplain, could you please call my sister for me? I'd really like to see her." I could have given John the money to make the call himself. But I got the impression he thought I would have some influence, since I was clergy. I did call. But I didn't have any influence. John's sister said she was busy and not interested in hearing about her brother.

I hope I'm not judging unfairly, but it seems to me that John's value as a person diminished with his lack of earning power. At least as far as his sister was concerned.

These are just two examples of how the world apart from God treats the helpless. The value we place on people will determine how we treat them. Much of the world pays homage to the rich and the powerful—those who have a lot to contribute to society. But people who are weak, poor, helpless, or "different" are ignored, abused, or cast aside.

Little People in the Big Apple

Living on Long Island, in a suburb of New York City, I see evidence of this abuse in our newspapers and TV programs.

Hear the word of the reporters.

Poor people are not treated as well as rich people. (How's that for a news flash?) Streets in the poorest sections of the city are the last to be plowed in the winter and the last to be repaired in the summer. Prices in their grocery stores are sometimes even higher than those in the affluent sections of the city.

A poor man sits in jail because he cannot raise a small bail for shoplifting, while a rich man can pay a several-thousand-dollar bail for grand larceny and walk in freedom until the trial.

There was a time when New York considered even poor people important. Remember the last census? Even the homeless were valuable then. Census takers searched high and low, trying to find everyone, even those who would normally be overlooked. Why? Because the Big Apple would lose millions in federal aid and seats in Congress if the census takers missed these normally overlooked people. For once, each person was of equal value. But it didn't last long. When the count was completed, life returned to "normal."

People have been bad-mouthing the poor at least since the time of Job. The Book of Job, which many scholars say is the earliest book written in the Bible, shows that many believed poverty and sickness were proof a person had sinned. Bildad said to Job, "If you are pure and upright, even now he [God] will rouse himself on your behalf and restore you to your rightful place" (Job 8:6).

Job's loss of possessions and health had made him an object of scorn among those who had once given him praise. In fact, the Book of Job was written to disprove the myth that health and wealth are related to righteousness.

Sometimes people are sick and poor for reasons beyond their control. And the last thing they need is to be ignored or given not-so-special treatment.

James 2 shows us that even the Early Church had a problem with favoritism. The rich got the good seats, the poor got the floor.

Sadly, even in churches today we sometimes treat the poor differently. We wouldn't be as blatant as to direct a person with fine clothes to a good seat, then instruct a poorly dressed person to stand. But does the poor person get invited into our homes as quickly? Do we give a warm welcome to the family with much to offer the church, then nearly ignore those with little to offer?

If we do, we follow the ways of the world and not the

ways of God. James is very plain when he says, "If you show favoritism, you sin" (2:9).

The Value of a Woman

Want a good example of how women in Bible times fared in the battle for equality with men?

Consider Lot.

He showed how much he valued his daughters when the men of Sodom surrounded his home and demanded he send out the male visitors for some impromptu sex. Lot said, "No, my friends. Don't do this wicked thing. Look, I have two daughters who have never slept with a man. Let me bring them out to you, and you can do what you like with them" (Genesis 19:7-8).

This is not an isolated incident. There's a similar story about a Levite and his concubine. A gang of men "raped her and abused her throughout the night" (Judges 19:25). The next morning the Levite found the woman dead on his doorstep. He was furious at the men who murdered her, but he did not take any blame for sending her to them.

No wonder a common prayer for Jewish men was to thank God they weren't a Gentile, a dog, or a woman. Since value in a primitive society depended on the ability to fight, physical strength was of great importance, and "weak women" were of little value.

But that was then. Now is now. We don't trash women today. Right?

When my daughter worked in the crisis care center of the Lamb's Club, a Nazarene ministry near Times Square, she and the other young women living there could not leave the building unescorted at night. And when my son taught composition at a well-known eastern university, he asked his students to write about their major concern on campus. The girls overwhelmingly wrote about their fear of walking on the campus Friday, Saturday, or Sunday nights when drinking lowered inhibitions and rapes were more common.

When there needs to be a hotline for abused women and safe houses for them to escape from their husbands and boyfriends, we are forced to admit that women are still being devalued.

Jesus devalued no one. He welcomed Mary as she sat at His feet and learned. And He did this in a day when it was not considered proper for a rabbi to teach a woman.

Jesus made sure His mother would be cared for, even as He hung on the Cross.

And He told Mary Magdalene to tell His disciples He was alive, even though in that day a woman was not considered a valid witness. In court, women were considered minors.

If we Christians are going to follow the example of Jesus, we need to teach and demonstrate the equality of women and men.

Majoring on the Minorities

Some people are devalued because of race. Our old immigration laws swung the doors open widest for northern Europeans. Immigrants with darker skin, who arrived in fewer numbers, faced problems associated with being different from those in the majority. (Would your great-great-grandfather have wanted to go into business with a short man from India who didn't speak English, or a newly freed slave who was an expert only in chopping cotton?)

Even with all our civil rights legislation, blacks are still discriminated against in housing, jobs, and opportunities. And too many Native Americans are still living on parched reservations.

Prejudice is an old problem, though. Even ancient Israel was prejudiced. "Dog" was a word Hebrews used to describe Gentiles. Israel even scorned the Samaritans, who worshiped God but who could not prove a pure Hebrew lineage. When Jesus asked a Samaritan woman for a drink, John 4:9 tells us she said, "'You are a Jew and I am a Samaritan woman. How can you ask me for a drink?' (For Jews do not associate with Samaritans.)"

To get Peter into the house of Cornelius, a Gentile, God had to send the apostle a vision. The Lord knew He had to break down this prejudice before the Church could grow.

Christians today need to again take the lead in accepting people of every race. And I think we're doing it. I see evidence of this in the New York district gatherings of my denomination, the Church of the Nazarene. At a recent assembly, people from 10 language groups were represented. Election to leadership positions reflected our diverse racial heritage.

One of the great truths of the New Testament is that followers of Jesus do not treat anyone as inferior.

"There is neither Jew nor Greek, slave nor free, male nor female, for you are all one in Christ Jesus" (Galatians 3:28).

This is a basic truth we need to believe and follow with everyone we meet. Every human being is a person for whom Jesus died. And everyone needs to be treated as such.

Ann Cubie Rearick is coordinator of pastoral care for Hospice Care of Long Island, Inc., and serves as associate pastor of the Massapequa Park Church of the Nazarene in New York.

Chapter 8

The Dragon of Materialism

by Stephen D. Eyre

Background Scripture: Matthew 6:24; Mark 10:17-25

AS I WRITE this chapter, I am in the process of buying a
new family car. How ironic. We do need a new car. Our third
child has just been born, and our old Chevette has 125,000
miles on it. Yet as I write about the dangers of preoccupation

with the abundance of possessions, I am preoccupied. I am making a purchase for which I will be paying for the next four years. It will stretch our budget to the limit.

As I struggle with this, I remind myself that possessions are not wrong in themselves. After all, God made the world for us to live in and enjoy. Nor can I draw a line and say, this much is all right and anything more is ungodly. That approach leads to a dangerous legalism. We must find an inner compass that can guide us through the numbing smog in which we are all engulfed. We must find a harness that can tame this dragon that enchants us.

The way materialism comes to occupy our hearts can be subtle. Initially we want to provide for ourselves and our family. The "standard package" is a three-bedroom house with central heating/air conditioning, two bathrooms, a dishwasher, and a garbage disposal. One car is a necessity, perhaps two. Yet to sustain such a standard life-style requires a great deal of energy from most of us. Usually the husband and wife both have to work. Living to work in order to buy becomes the family preoccupation.

After all, what is wrong with seeking to realize the American dream? Isn't it our right? But after all our effort, we have little time or energy left to consider the spiritual aspects of life. While believing there is more to life than owning and possessing, buying and possessing becomes the hub of our lives. The dragon of materialism moves into our hearts and unpacks his bags.

The Gospel of Prosperity

The dragon of materialism has moved into the church in blatant ways. Many Christians believe that God's blessings mean material prosperity for all who ask for them. The gospel, behind the flame of this dragon, becomes the gospel of prosperity.

Appealing to the materialistic infection of our hearts, one author writes, "Prosperity is yours! It is not something you have to strive to work toward. *You Have a Title Deed to Prosperity.* Jesus bought and paid for your prosperity just like He bought and paid for your healing and your salvation."[1] Or as another characterized it, "God's got it, I can have it, and by faith I'm going to get it."[2]

How can these people honestly believe this? I think to myself. Don't they see what the Scriptures say about the choice between serving God or money? However, I must confess they are only saying what I want to believe.

The church for most of its 2,000 years has warned against the dangers of materialism. Bernard of Clairvaux wrote in the 12th century, "Money no more satisfies the hunger of the mind than air supplies the body's need for bread."[3]

The flip side of the gospel of prosperity is the gospel of simple living. For a period in my life I reacted to the materialism of the world and the church by refusing to buy much of anything. Authentic Christians, I thought, should be committed to owning as little as possible. Living in the most inexpensive housing available and owning a limited wardrobe and an old car were what I considered Christian essentials. At one time I even refused to buy a washing machine and dryer even when we had two children in diapers.

While my wife, Jackie, was spending every other day at the Laundromat, a couple of family friends took me aside for a frank talk on caring for my family. As I struggled with the issue of materialism, I discovered that I was still being materialistic. I was measuring my spirituality and the spirituality of others by how much or how little they owned.

The Dangers

The real problem of materialism is that it blinds us to the spiritual aspects of reality. It destroys the spiritual roots of our lives.

The dragon of materialism leads us to become preoccupied with the material side of life. All our time, energy, and thought are focused on the physical aspects of life. We become practical materialists. We know that there is more to life, but the way we live shows that we have adopted the creed of the dragon of materialism: "Matter is all that matters."

Our experience of life in Christ becomes hollow. Our knowledge of God becomes empty. If we can't see it, taste it, touch it, smell it, or measure it, then we doubt that it's real; therefore, we come to doubt that God is real.

Worldly Salvation

Jesus, knowing what materialism does to us, warned against believing that our lives consist of an abundance of possessions. He told a rich young ruler that eternal life was available to him only if he sold all he had and then followed (Mark 10:17-22). He warned the disciples that it was easier for a camel to go through the eye of a needle than for a rich man to enter the kingdom of God (vv. 23-25). He warned against storing up treasures on earth (Matthew 6:19). He warned that one could gain the whole world and in the process lose his own soul (16:26).

Despite the warnings, the infection of materialism is so pervasive that even those of us who don't consciously believe in a gospel of material prosperity live it in a subtle way. Don't we measure the blessing of God by the balance in our checkbook? Don't we evaluate the success of a ministry by the size of its building? Don't we judge the power of a church by the size of its budget? Don't we measure a church's concern for others by the size of its missions budget?

It is hard for spiritual riches to compete with material ones. On a daily basis, I must admit, I am more preoccupied with working to put money in the bank than I am with following Jesus' admonition to store up treasure in heaven.

Remember the game of Monopoly? The object is to go around the board in order to buy property and earn money. As the game progresses, money and deeds begin to be monopolized by one or two players. Those who are getting monopolies are having a great time and are in no hurry for the game to end. However, if you happen to have only a few deeds and little money, the game begins to drag on and on. You begin to look forward to the end so you can get on with something else. Likewise, as long as we have hope that we can win in this life, the promise that we will have blessings in the heavenlies seems to lack something (Ephesians 1:3).

Jesus rebuked the church at Laodicea for its material affluence and its spiritual ignorance. Surely He rebukes us. "You say, 'I am rich; I have acquired wealth and do not need a thing.' But you do not realize that you are wretched, pitiful, poor, blind and naked" (Revelation 3:17).

I feel bad for those of us who have lost spiritual awareness. I don't want that for myself or for God's people. I want my life to be filled with His presence. I want a living faith, full of spiritual life that will allow me to be with God throughout my day.

An awareness of a spiritual reality alters forever the way we live and view the world. We understand that the quantity of our possessions does not make the quality of our lives. We see that preoccupation with an earthly existence can rob us of true spiritual experience. With spiritual strength we seek spiritual growth.

---

1. Gloria Copeland, *God's Will Is Prosperity* (Tulsa, Okla.: Harrison House, 1978), 46.

2. Os Guinness, *The Gravedigger File* (Downers Grove, Ill.: InterVarsity Press, 1983), 132.

3. Bernard of Clairvaux, "On the Love of God," *Late Medieval Mysticism,* ed. Ray Petry (Philadelphia: Westminster Press, 1957), 59.

Stephen D. Eyre is an author and a campus staff worker with Inter-Varsity students in England. This chapter is taken from *Defeating the Dragons of the World,* by Stephen D. Eyre. © 1987 by Inter-Varsity Christian Fellowship of the USA and used by permission of InterVarsity Press, P.O. Box 1400, Downers Grove, IL 60515.

Chapter 9

Success:
In Search of the Secret

by Beth Fisher Watkins

Background Scripture: 2 Chronicles 26:1-21; Luke 6:20;
10:20

WE'RE A CULTURE of yuppies, buppies, and dinks.[1]
Even the labels we give ourselves reflect our obsession with
making money and moving up the employment ladder.

With the fervor of Ponce de Leon searching for the
Fountain of Youth, we explore every path that might lead to
the secret of success. Unfortunately, we often end up at
small springs. Though they may be wonderful to look at and

refreshing to drink from, they don't bubble forth the elixir we are hoping for.

I've been disappointed at a spring or two. And I've watched and listened as others, thinking they've found the true fountain, have shared their routes to success.

A Little Advice

My father recently pulled me aside and told me the first five years of my career are crucial to professional success. We stood in the basement, surrounded by stored furniture and boxes of our family's history. As we discussed the condition and fate of my infant crib, Dad warned me about one of the most common mistakes young professionals make: getting caught too early in the brier of family responsibilities.

Some employers send out a clear message that family responsibilities at any point in your career are roadblocks on the path to success. Multi-billionaire industrialist H. Ross Perot seems to be looking for employees willing to put everything second to their career—family included. He told one interviewer, "I want people who love the battlefield, people willing to go to the wall."

A report in the *Harvard Business Review* told of companies that promote "career-primary" women and penalize "career-and-family" women, those equally interested in careers and having children.

A *Kansas City Times* article on men, careers, and family said, "When a man goes public with his decision to make family a priority, he had better have a strong and anchored ego to withstand the reaction he is likely to experience."[2]

I enjoy my career, but I doubt I'm willing to sacrifice parenthood for professional success.

No need, says Al Neuharth, founder of *USA Today* and former chairman of Gannett. The real secret to success is failure. "Everyone should fail in a big way at least once before they're forty. I don't mean little disappointments ... It needs to be a big failure. You can only fail big if you take a big risk. The bigger you fail, the bigger you are likely to succeed later."[3]

I'm confused about how I should use this bit of wisdom. I understand the concept of taking risks, but I'm not about to openly invite failure.

On a recent trip, while flipping through an in-flight magazine, I came across another baffling bit of advice on success: For a woman to succeed in business, she must make people forget she is a woman for eight hours of the day, and make sure they remember she is a woman the rest of the time.

I'm still scratching my head.

Still more confusing are the claims of proponents of the "theology of success." They say God has promised to bless Christians with prosperity. Their secret to success is a simple formula: Ask and receive.

That theory is a little unnerving to me. God has not blessed me with great financial or material success, though I've asked. But perhaps I was asking for the wrong thing. It seems possible, given scriptures like Luke 6:20: "Blessed are you who are poor, for yours is the kingdom of God." And let's not forget James 1:2: "Consider it pure joy . . . whenever you face trials of many kinds." I assume James means financial difficulty too.

All this advice leaves me confused.

But this I'm sure of: I wish I knew the secret to worldly success. It appeals to me. If there is any way to remain a Christian and still achieve worldly success, I'd like both.

I'd like a high-powered job, a high-powered car, and a high-priced home.

But I have yet to find the secret to that sort of success. And I struggle with my views of success in light of the kind of success Jesus wants me to pursue.

Jesus the Failure

In terms of renown, Jesus is one of the most successful

people who ever lived. He certainly has notoriety. Some 2,000 years after He walked this earth, His name is still a household word. His wisdom is still quoted. His people-managing skills are revered. Each week, millions of His followers gather to learn about Him and worship Him.

But if we hold Jesus up to current standards of success, He was a failure. Not only was His home worth less than the median price for those in His day—He didn't have a home. Conceived out of wedlock, He was part of what we might call a "dysfunctional family." Many of His followers were considered undesirables: lepers, tax collectors, prostitutes, and the like. His closest associates abandoned Him. From the time He was an infant, people plotted to kill Him. And they finally succeeded. He died a criminal's death and was buried in a borrowed tomb. In death, He was left without even His clothes, which the soldiers at the Cross divided among themselves.

Most of us would shudder to think that Jesus would require us to be hated and persecuted in the ways He was. But if we are to be successful in being Christlike, what is required of us?

An ancient yuppie asked that question of Jesus. If the conversation were replayed in our times, it might sound like this:[4]

"Jesus, what good thing should I do to get eternal life?"

"Obey the commandments."

"Which commandments?" the young professional asks.

"Do not murder, do not commit adultery, do not steal, do not give false testimony, honor your father and mother . . ."

With each commandment, the young man nods impatiently.

". . . and 'love your neighbor as yourself.' "

"I've done all those things, but I feel like something is missing."

Jesus answers, "If you want to be successful in following

me, go, sell your possessions and give the money to the poor, and you will have treasure in heaven. Then come, follow me."

Shoulders slump, eyes fall, and the young man turns to walk away. I can almost hear him muttering, "Not my new sailboat. Besides, I've used it to take the church youth group sailing. I couldn't do without my house, either. Giving my home away would be too radical. Where would I sleep? How would I live? I don't understand what He means by 'treasure in heaven,' but I do know that for now I have to live in *this* world. I can't be an effective witness if everyone thinks I'm a fanatic."

Boston Calling

The story of the rich young ruler has bothered me since I was a child. I've heard it used many times as an argument against worldly success and possessions. But a few years ago, I began to see the true meaning of the principles Jesus shared with the young ruler. The young man wasn't asked to give up success because it was success, but because it kept him from following Jesus.

I was a college student, majoring in music performance. As an accomplished flutist, I had big dreams of being a professional musician. I was in constant competition and reveled in each victory. A year earlier, I had the honor of being recognized as the best high school flutist in the state and had performed several solos in a statewide recital.

I felt the Boston Pops calling me, or so I thought. I spent four or five hours each day in a tiny practice room, watching myself in an oval mirror to correct my stance and embouchure (the formation of the musician's lips and mouth while playing a wind instrument). Each week, I traveled many miles to take private lessons and work with performance groups.

The pulpit of my father's church was one of my favorite performance spots, because it helped me believe the deceit that I was using my talent for the Lord. I found opportunity to play my showiest pieces and preface them with vague spiritual ties.

But somewhere along the line I asked the same question the rich young ruler did. Knowing I had kept the commandments, I probed further and asked, "What is missing?" And Jesus pointed to my success as a musician and said, "This is what keeps you from succeeding as a Christian. Give it up and follow Me."

But I shook my head and walked away, mumbling, "Not my music. I almost have it made. Besides, I've used it for Your glory too."

I struggled for months. I began each practice session, staring at the same mirror in that same tiny room, with a desperate prayer. Hands folded around my silver-plated flute, I'd say, "God, help me give You the glory." But practicing was difficult; my technique faltered; my confidence waned. And I finally submitted to the realization this wasn't the success God wanted me to pursue. Reluctantly, I packed away my music, my flute, and my dream.

I floundered with time on my hands and no dream to pursue. I took on a secretarial job and learned to type. The next fall, I heard the yearbook was short-staffed, so I volunteered. I had given up the dream of musical success, but I felt as if I was just marking time. If Jesus wanted me to follow Him, why wasn't He showing me the path?

Gradually my interest in the yearbook grew into a fascination with journalism. I delved into newspapers, carefully watched the news, analyzed magazines, and began to notice the lack of Christian professionals in journalism.

I left the Christian college campus and enrolled at a state university with a highly respected journalism school. God showed me that music wasn't the only talent I had that could be shared. I've developed a conviction to use my writing abilities in Christian publications, or perhaps as a Christian influence in the secular media.

By the world's standards, I'm not always a successful editor. Because of my workload, I disappoint my writers by holding their manuscripts, with no comments, for months at a time. I disappoint my supervisors by missing deadlines. And I feel like I disappoint my readers by not giving more time to the articles I edit.

But I don't disappoint Jesus. For when I asked, "What is missing?" He said, "Give up your idea of success and follow Me." And I did.

Give It All Away?

Does biblical success have to mean failure by the world's standards? Is there any place for powerful businesspersons, popular artists, political leaders, or celebrity preachers in this idea of biblical success?

The Bible gives us plenty of examples of men who were successful in both God's eyes and the world's eyes; Joseph, David, and Solomon are three of the best known. But these weren't self-made men. They were each forged and formed by God. For each of them, their success in the world's eyes took second place to their desire for success in God's eyes. And in each case, their worldly success was the result of God's presence in their lives. (See Genesis 39:23; 1 Samuel 18:14; 1 Chronicles 22:11-13.)

There are also examples in the Bible of people who let worldly success go to their head. Uzziah was a young, upwardly mobile professional. At 16, he became the king of Judah, and he reigned for 52 years. As long as he looked to the Lord in his decision making, he was successful (2 Chronicles 26:5). But as his success and power grew, he outgrew God. He forgot he was a God-made man, not a self-made one.

One day, he decided he had the right to burn incense in the Temple. After all, he was the king. But this was a job reserved for priests. God struck him with leprosy for his arrogance, and the king remained a leper until he died (vv. 16-21).

Success can go to our head in the ministry too. Remember when Jesus sent out the 72? They returned thrilled with their success. "Lord, even the demons submit to us in your name" (Luke 10:17).

Jesus replied, "Do not rejoice that the spirits submit to you, but rejoice that your names are written in heaven" (v. 20).

It seems easy to lose sight of that heavenly success when we're living in this world, where success means top-notch jobs, top-of-the-line cars, and all the other fixin's. Jim Bakker did. Jimmy Swaggart did. And so have you and I.

Most of the world sees success as getting ahead, being a leader. But Jesus asks us to give up that idea and be a successful follower.

When I become discouraged with my job and am tempted to believe I've failed both myself and God, I sometimes wonder what I could have accomplished as a professional musician. In those moments, I can almost hear the orchestra warming up, the white noise of crowd chatter beyond the stage curtain, and the swell of applause as the curtain is lifted. And I start to wish I could be waiting in the wings instead of battling deadlines in my office.

Where I sit, I don't hear much applause. Yet I'm trying to base my idea of success not on human praise but on heavenly approval. And when I think about that, I can almost hear the faint strums of a harp, the echoes of a heavenly choir, and a warm and welcome voice singing, "Well done."

---

1. Yuppies = Young Urban Professionals; Buppies = Black Urban Professionals; Dinks = Double Income, No Kids.
2. Aimee Lee Ball, "Career or Family? Fathers Face Choice, Too," *Kansas City Times* (November 22, 1989).

3. Al Neuharth, "Fail Big to Win Big," *Marriott PORTFOLIO* (March/April 1990), 14-16.

4. See Matthew 19:16-22.

Beth Watkins is an editor in the Adult Ministries Department at Church of the Nazarene International Headquarters, Kansas City.

Chapter 10

How Christians Should Use Power

by Tom Barnard

Background Scripture: John 13:12-17; Philippians 2:5-11

OUR THREE-YEAR-OLD granddaughter, Lyndsay, looked perplexed. A talkative, inquiring child, she examined the five-inch piece of bent plastic.

"Papa," she asked me, "is this mine?"

"No," I replied, "it's Papa's."

She turned it over in her tiny hands, exploring it more carefully.

"What is it?" she asked.

"Well, it's called a shoehorn."

"Oh," she responded. "Blow it."

I turned away, trying to hide the laughter building within me. For Lyndsay, it was an introduction to double meanings. For me, it was one of those special moments I would tell others about for days.

Multiple-meaning words. Our language is full of them. *Power* is one of those words. Power can be good, or it can be bad.

Standing alone, it is incomplete. The word begs for a modifier. So we give it what it seems to need.

Nuclear power. Political power. Manpower. Horsepower. Black power. White power.

Add a preposition and we create a new dimension. Power of persuasion. Power of money. Power of the press. Power of positive thinking. Power of prayer.

But Christians know about the many kinds of power. What confuses many is how to use power and stay Christian. But before we consider how to use it, let's look at how not to use it.

Power Gone Sour

"Sesame Street" did a spoof of the classic *Tale of Two Cities*, by Charles Dickens. They called it *A Tale of Two Breakfasts*. Ernie's opening words to Bert were, "It was the best of oatmeals, it was the worst of oatmeals." I can almost hear Dickens groan.

But the point is that many good things in the world have a bad side. Any given day may be a good one for a rich person and a bad one for a homeless person. One hungry person may get smooth oatmeal, while another gets it lumpy.

One person may enjoy power, while another suffers from it.

If you conducted a word-association test using *power,* you might generate words like *command, leverage, drive, control, strength, and force.*

By themselves, the words sound great. They are perfectly acceptable. How can an army advance without command? How could one person alone move a giant rock without leverage? How can a salesperson succeed without drive? How can a chief executive officer lead a meeting without control?

But each of these power terms can also point to different forms of torture.

Command can lead to psychological abuse. Leverage can become manipulation. Drive can give way to winning at any cost. Control can lead to gaining an unfair advantage.

There is an executive in a religious organization for whom control is job one. At least that's the observation some of his employees have made. He manages an office of around 50 people.

He recently had to construct a policy to solve a problem that affected not only his office but his entire organization. He decided on a policy he knew would not have the support of his subordinate department heads. So rather than involve them by seeking their insights and expertise about the problem, he worked the policy out on his own. Unfortunately, his solution had not been discussed. And, as a lone maverick, he had no way of anticipating some of the expensive implications of his solution. Nor did his supervisors know enough about the problem to ask the right questions when the solution was proposed.

As a result, they bought the proposal. And now the entire organization is paying the price in dwindling customers and low morale.

For generations, philosophers and social scientists have been explaining that human behavior is related to any number of drives with which people become obsessed—drives like hunger, sex, and ambition.

Few philosophers affected the world more profoundly than German philosopher Friedrich Nietzsche. Although he wrote his most important works before the end of the 19th century, his influence reached a peak after World War I.

It was his radical views that attracted young Fascists in Italy and their Nazi counterparts during the 1930s.

Nietzsche taught that strength was the ultimate virtue and weakness the only sin. He argued that it is power—not faith or reason—that determines the destiny of people and nations. He said the human desire for power is basic to life, and exploitation of others is as natural as life itself.

"Exploitation does not belong to a depraved, or imperfect and primitive society," he wrote. "It belongs to the nature of the living being as a primary organic function; it is a consequence of the intrinsic Will to Power, which is precisely the Will to Life" (*Beyond Good and Evil* [Macmillan Co., 1909], 9:259).

This is an atheist's-eye view of the world. And it is not out of step with our society today. Even in our modern world, long after Charles Darwin first wrote about evolution and the survival of the fittest, we still hear the echoes of humanity's struggle for existence.

In this streetwise secular world not only is it considered acceptable to manipulate, coerce, exploit, suppress, injure, and conquer the weak, but it is the smart thing to do. In the battle for life and success, only the strong survive.

It is not goodness we honor with high salaries, perks, and praise; it is strength. It is not humility we reward, but the evidence of pride. Unselfishness is out; unrestrained egotism is in.

Some of the world's most visible heroes—athletes, actors, musicians, millionaires, entrepreneurs, and even televangelists—have been revealed as people who go to evil lengths to get what they want.

In a recent biography of one Hollywood actor, the author points out the man's flaws (vanity, selfishness, excessive ego) but stresses the man's strengths (charm, versatility, and intelligence). The actor's success seems to suggest our world allows for trade-offs that make some sin acceptable when balanced against the contribution the person makes to society.

You can almost hear a fan defending the actor. "Sure he has character flaws, but who doesn't? Look at the entertainment he has given millions, and the good he has done for animal rights and the environment. It is the bottom line that counts."

A non-Christian perspective of power is a survival perspective. It is based on:

> bottom-line results
> priority of ideas over people
> accountability to self
> elimination of rules
> survival of the fittest

Power to Serve

So much for the "worst of oatmeals," that is, the worst side of the power issue. But can there really be a best side? If Lord Acton's old saying is true, "Power tends to corrupt," why waste time talking about a Christian perspective of power? Why not just sum up the advice in two words: "Avoid power"?

The problem is that empowerment words aren't limited to business manuals on how to get ahead through ruthlessness. They're in the Bible too. Both the Old and New Testaments.

For example, when Bible writers describe God, they talk about His omnipotence—His power.

Scriptures speak of God's "great power and mighty strength" (Isaiah 40:26); "the power of [His] awesome works" (Psalm 145:6); the power by which He created the earth (Jeremiah 10:12).

New Testament writers said Jesus shared this same quality of power.

"The Son is the radiance of God's glory and the exact representation of his being, sustaining all things by his powerful word" (Hebrews 1:3). "He was with God in the beginning. Through him all things were made; without him nothing was made that has been made" (John 1:2-3).

But Jesus gave new meaning to the word "power."

Paul wrote, "Who, being in very nature God, did not consider equality with God something to be grasped, but made himself nothing, taking the very nature of a servant, being made in human likeness" (Philippians 2:6-7).

Jesus walked through life as each of us does—as a child, as a teenager, as a young adult—experiencing the same stages of development common to all humanity. He grew, He learned, He matured. To do this, He had to relinquish His divine power and leave His throne in heaven. By His example, Jesus calls us to relinquish our power and to discover strength in weakness rather than in intimidation and control.

Jesus came to deliver God's power to believers through His Spirit. It is not our human powers that are blessed and cleansed for God's use. The power Christians receive comes from God.

Before the Day of Pentecost, Jesus told the disciples to "wait for the gift my Father promised" (Acts 1:4). That gift from God would be accompanied by signs and wonders, and the disciples would be empowered to be His witnesses. It was not the demonstration of human power the disciples celebrated on the Day of Pentecost. It was the power of God.

Paul wrote to his friends in Ephesus, "I pray also that . . . you may know the hope to which he has called you . . . and his incomparably great power for us who believe" (Ephesians 1:18-19). The power that dominates in the Book of Acts is the power that accompanies the presence of the Holy Spirit in the lives of believers.

Jesus came to show that true power comes through serving others. His kingdom is a kingdom of servants. To enter His kingdom, we must be willing to love, to submit, to obey, to surrender, to yield, to practice humility, to consider others first.

The week of His death, Jesus astonished His disciples by leaving the supper table and washing their feet. The group sat in stunned silence as the Master Servant washed the feet of His followers. When He was finished, Jesus said, "You call me 'Teacher' and 'Lord,' and rightly so, for that is what I am. Now that I, your Lord and Teacher, have washed your feet, you also should wash one another's feet. I have set you an example that you should do as I have done for you" (John 13:13-15).

For the Christian, power and service are inseparable.

One more thought. I believe that the more we have of human power, the less we have of spiritual power. During one of Paul's testing times, he received from God what he called a thorn in the flesh. He prayed earnestly for its removal. The Lord offered grace instead, saying to Paul, "My power is made perfect in weakness" (2 Corinthians 12:9). And Paul replied, "I will boast all the more gladly about my weaknesses, so that Christ's power may rest on me. . . . For when I am weak, then I am strong" (vv. 9-10).

When we discover our human limitations, we can also discover the unlimited grace and power of God.

I have a friend whose craving for the good life led him to break a fair number of federal laws. At the advice of his attorneys he pleaded guilty to a reduced number of counts and was sentenced to serve about three years in prison.

Months before he entered prison, he surrendered his will to God. His life had bottomed out, and he realized the only way he could ever face his family and friends was to present them with a new man who had been changed by the

Lord. Shortly after being locked up, my friend wrote, apologetically, "I wish I could give you answers to questions I'm sure you have, but I am still wrestling with the questions myself."

In the same letter he wrote, "I pray I am finally broken to where God can use me to produce that which will endure. If so, it only took me 20 years—that's half the time it took Jacob or Moses."

His was not the typical "jail-house Christianity." He volunteered his time to the prison chaplain, led Bible studies, preached, organized evangelistic services, led fellow prisoners to the Lord, and counseled them in the Christian walk.

As a result, my friend discovered that the power to lead others came when he began serving others. In addition, the peace and satisfaction he did not achieve through human power became his through surrendering those powers to the Lordship of Jesus Christ.

He is out of prison now and back with his family. Together they are engaged in a full-time ministry to the socially powerless. Reflecting on his stay in prison, my friend wrote, "I think that a few months in prison should be part of the required training for *all* ministers."

Paul would probably agree with him.

Prayer:
Lord, teach me to be submissive rather than assertive, obedient rather than demanding. Help me be responsive to those who are hurting, rather than to be judgmental and rude. Prompt me to seek Your leadership in my life, rather than trust my human instincts. Help me understand that the only empowerment that really matters in life is that which accompanies the presence of Your Spirit within me. And, Lord, open doors of opportunity for me to be a servant to others. Amen.

Tom Barnard is vice president of Eastern Nazarene College, Quincy, Mass.

Chapter 11

Is Anything Ever Wrong Anymore?

by Roger L. Hahn

Background Scripture: Exodus 20:1-17; Luke 6:31

THERE IS A TIME TO BE BORN, and a time to die. So says the writer of Ecclesiastes.

In between these, according to the accepted practice of our age,

> there is a time to lie and a time to be honest,
> a time to murder and a time to save lives,
> a time to abort and a time to give birth,
> a time to insult and a time to encourage,
> a time to manipulate and a time to cooperate,
> a time to steamroll and a time to tiptoe.

This is called relativism—the belief that everything is relative, depending on the situation; nothing is always wrong. Even the Ten Commandments is up for grabs.

We know that people outside the church preach relativism. But their sermons are reaching into the church and changing the lives of Christians.

I know a young pastor who was stunned when a friend accused him of adultery. "Oh, no," the pastor responded, "I'm not committing adultery. I'm just in love with two women."

The friend answered, "That's what the Bible calls adultery."

"No," the pastor replied in a confused voice. "Adultery is a sin, and I haven't sinned." At least it didn't feel like sin to him. As is too often the case for pastors, the path to adultery began during pastoral counseling sessions. There, the pastor and parishioner shared intimate words to identify and heal heartache. Words gave way to touches, and touches gave way to adultery.

It all happened so naturally, and the couple's shared feelings were so genuine that the pastor said, "It's as if God led us into this."

But would that have been the same God who said, "You shall not commit adultery" (Exodus 20:14)?

I know another Christian who gave in to the world's preaching on relativism. Actually, she was won over by the practice of relativism she saw in her church.

"They are all hypocrites," the young lady told a colleague of mine. The lady was a first-year student in the Christian college at which I teach. My colleague was her adviser.

"Who are the hypocrites?" her adviser asked.

"All of them. My parents, my pastor, my Sunday School teacher, the church board members, the youth minister—they're all hypocrites. My dad's on the church board, but he drinks at the company parties."

The adviser knew what was coming, but he asked the question anyway. "What has that got to do with you? Why did you sneak out of the dorm and spend the night at your boyfriend's apartment?"

"If nobody else obeys the rules," she said, "don't think I'm going to obey either!"

This lady never had a course in ethics. She never sat in classes where teachers and students analyzed relativism and situational ethics. But she had grown up in a holiness church. She had listened to plenty of teaching and preaching about right and wrong. She had heard plenty of lectures at home about rights and wrongs. But when she saw her parents and respected members of the church choosing to disregard some teachings of the church, moral confusion set in.

If they had the right to choose which things they considered right and which things they considered wrong, so did she.

She had no training that would have helped her think through the dangerous consequences of her actions. She had not considered whether social drinking for members of a church that forbids it has the same moral consequences as casual sex.

Her conclusion was simple. "If my parents can do whatever they want to, so can I." The result was clear. She no longer believed in moral absolutes. She no longer believed that some things are absolutely wrong, always.

These two cases are not the only examples of the creeping relativism invading the church. They are not even the worst examples I've seen.

Christianity has always taught there are some moral absolutes. Certain behavior will always be right, and certain behavior will always be wrong.

But the world apart from Christ has come to the conclusion nothing is always right or always wrong. Rightness and wrongness are relative to the situation. What is especially distressing is how rapidly this relativism is invading the church.

Roots of a Warped Teaching

The roots of the philosophy of relativism run 200 years deep, to the period known as the Enlightenment. This was a time philosophers began rejecting church authority. These keen thinkers believed they could discover all truth, including matters of right and wrong, through human reason.

Logic became the final authority, bumping aside the authority of the Word and will of God.

Then, about a hundred years ago, Sigmund Freud began teaching that sexual experiences of children programs their behavior in later life. This complicated the issue of right and wrong. How could it be wrong for a man to lie, if this tendency was programmed into him during his infancy?

Other theories of psychology followed. As a result, among psychologists outside the religious community, human behavior is rarely thought of as right or wrong. And the rest of society is buying into this. We are beginning to think, speak, and act as if a person's behavior is the result of something other than a choice that person made. Instead, we are rationalizing that their behavior was caused by early childhood experiences, poor relationships with their mother, or some other psychological trauma in their history. Right and wrong disappears. Behavior is tied directly to one's past experiences.

Perhaps one reason relativism is so popular today is because it allows people the freedom to ignore the God of Scripture. For it is impossible to believe in moral absolutes without also believing in a God who reveals that some things are always right and some things are always wrong.

If It Works, It's OK

Few folks today worry about the philosophical background of relativism. But we live in a world that has no moral foundation because of these developments in human thought. And as a result of this fact, most folks make decisions on the basis of what works, what feels good, or what is easiest.

Not a great many people these days make decisions by asking, "What is the right thing to do?" The consequences are staggering.

For a full generation the world has been urging people to make decisions about sexual conduct on the basis of what feels good at the moment. The AIDS epidemic is only the most-publicized result. To the list of consequences we must add broken relationships, loneliness, disillusionment, boredom and impotency in sexual activity, pornography, sexual abuse, and increased homosexuality.

"If it ain't broken, don't fix it" is a North American truism. You can translate that phrase, "If it works, it's right." Some nations that do business with us consider this a hallmark of America. However, when this truism is applied to decisions of right and wrong, the consequences can be disastrous.

For example, what works when an unplanned and unwanted pregnancy interferes with a person's career, freedom, or reputation? Well, what works to keep the career, freedom, and reputation is an abortion.

"The easy way is the right way." This is another popular viewpoint today. Most of us are in a hurry. If there is a shortcut to our goal, we should take it regardless of whether it is right or wrong. If you want to outrace the world's fastest human and set a record, illegal steroids will get you to the finish line quicker.

The world apart from Christ is confused about right and wrong. How much worse is this confusion when the church falls into the grip of the same moral decay?

The young pastor in love with both his wife and a woman he was counseling did not believe in moral relativism. He had been taught, he believed, he preached that the Word and will of God identify some things, including adultery, as always wrong. Six months earlier he would have reacted with horror at the idea that he would commit adultery.

But the pervasive influence of the world—the repeated teaching that if it *feels* right, it *is* right—had dulled his moral sensitivity. He had joked enough about infidelity. He had seen enough references to extramarital sex on TV. So when Wrong led him step-by-step down a gradual incline, he didn't realize where he was headed until he arrived on the threshold. None of the small steps seemed wrong. In fact, each step felt right. He was genuinely shocked when he finally realized the truth of his error.

Moral relativism of our worldly culture has crept into the lives of church people. There's no question about that. The question is, what are we going to do about it?

What the Church Can Do

The church can confidently and frequently remind people that there are moral absolutes.

The Ten Commandments and the Golden Rule are not moral options. We can't take them or leave them, depending on what works for us, what feels good, or what is most convenient. They are expressions of God's ultimate will: a will that always favors love of God and neighbor over love of self.

The church ought to admit it is not always easy to figure out how to live out these moral absolutes. Sometimes we have to choose between the lesser of two evils. For example, if someone breaks into your house and threatens to kill you, should you kill them if you get a chance?

These dilemmas do not mean we should become moral relativists. When we face two evils, we should call both evil. And our choice of the lesser of the two should be made with godly sorrow and repentance. We confuse people, especially young ones, when we reduce difficult issues to simplistic statements. And we further confound them when we call evil good just because it may be less evil than some other option. Our involvement in World War II was not made good because it helped stop the evil of the Holocaust. But fighting, as opposed to standing idly by, seemed the better option—at least for many Christians.

The church has been the main voice proclaiming moral absolutes in the years past. But in recent years it seems the church is becoming more interested in success and comfort, more interested in what works than in what is right.

We have not stopped speaking of moral absolutes. We just speak less often and with less conviction. This can be fatal.

The voice of the world without Christ is becoming louder and more penetrating every day. Christians need to respond, because the longest, loudest voice is the voice that is heard.

In a way, we stand in a crowd. Some are yelling for the crucifixion of moral absolutes. Others need to be yelling for the life of those absolutes.

Perhaps part of the young pastor's problem was that he heard the wrong crowd over the godly crowd.

However, matters of right and wrong are not learned only by hearing the words of others. We learn not to lie both by being taught not to lie and by seeing our parents and other loved ones refusing to lie even when it is easier than telling the truth.

Right moral decisions come from practicing right moral decisions. Practice makes perfect. Young people learn to make right moral choices by being partners with parents and friends who are making right moral choices.

Years ago we spoke about holiness of heart *and life*. We've come to a point where many think holiness of heart is a private, internal matter. And it is. But if holiness of heart is not accompanied by a holiness of life that stands up under the examination of the absolutes of God, then there is no holiness of heart. All that is left is a creeping relativism, and a future in which nothing is ever really wrong anymore.

Roger Hahn is an associate professor of religion at Southern Nazarene University, Bethany, Okla.

Chapter 12

Now for Something Good
About the World:
It Keeps Us Honest

by Geoff Gorsuch

Background Scripture: Matthew 5:44-47; 23:1-3, 5-7, 23

THE CABDRIVER turned around, barely controlling his anger. He sneered at me through tobacco-stained teeth. "How does that help me pay the bills?"

His cynical rejection hurt, and suddenly I was on the defensive. And rightfully so. "Here and now" was this man's credo. The so-called testimony I had just given spoke only of "there and then."

The cabdriver didn't care about eternal life, church, blessings, or heaven. Religion and its rituals just didn't interest him. He was too honest—too real—to feel the need for spiritual indulgence. Salvation from the bill collectors was his primary concern. He was looking for practical help in attaining a certain amount of dignity in this life—not the next.

Far from the church and a foreigner to its Christian worldview, here was secular man at his finest. Brutally honest.

The problem wasn't his. Preoccupied with making a living, raising the kids, and pleasing his wife, he simply could not see the relevance of anything that couldn't help him with all that.

The problem was mine. I hadn't seen him as a fellow human being with all the struggles and needs of a man. He needed a genuine, "How's it going?" and a listening ear. All I had given him was, "Let me tell you." Or worse, "Hasn't Jesus been good to me?" (Why hadn't He been good to him?) I had been answering questions he was not asking.

What he wanted was to see God "fleshed out" in the midst of the pressing realities of his daily life. He wanted models that worked, not rituals that didn't. All he had heard from me was a self-justifying and rather shallow theology of affluence.

Hypocrisy, words without deeds that express genuine love, has never been able to withstand the world's test of logic. For secular man, now more than ever, the messenger is the message. Though this concept surprises us, it is not news to God! "The Word became flesh and made his dwelling among us. We have seen his glory . . . full of grace and truth" (John 1:14).

Get Real

Throughout the Bible, God calls His children to greater authenticity and challenges the teachings and practices of the religious establishment. Consider Christ's final evaluation of the religious institutions of His day. "They do not practice what they preach. . . . You give a tenth of your spices . . . But you have neglected the more important matters of the law—justice, mercy and faithfulness" (Matthew 23:3, 23).

Christ challenged the hypocrisy of His day. And that cost Him His life. Today, by challenging what we call God or godliness and our traditions, the secular man brings us back to God by keeping us honest. He forces us to think. He prods us to find newer and fresher expressions of the proven truths of Scripture: "new wineskins." He forces us to reflect on what the Cross means for us today, here and now.

Perhaps that is why we see neither Jesus nor Paul attacking the Caesar cult, the sexually perverted polytheism, or the pseudosophistication of the day in order to verify the message. They probably knew that the seeds of those movements' destruction had already been sown.

Instead, we see them putting the accent on self-sacrificial love, and in light of that, confronting hypocrisy in their own ranks. It was in reference to the Temple itself that Christ preached, "You have a fine way of setting aside the commands of God in order to observe your own traditions!" (Mark 7:9). The issue was authenticity. Self-justifying public ritual excused the lack of personal obedience. And it's the same today.

The Cost of Authenticity

The church has begun to deny the central teaching of Christianity and its most important symbol of authenticity —the Cross. Christ became involved in this world to the point of pain. So should authentic Christians today.

Life, instead, has become a game. And this attitude usually leads to trifling. We do a little of this, a little of that, and we overlook the emotional investments necessary to build a future for ourselves and our children. Religion is reduced to a personal inner experience that has absolutely no bearing on our daily behavior.

It is how we face our daily responsibilities that is the mark of a Christian, not the "Christian activities" we do. Discipleship is not coming up with another gimmick for marketing the message. It's developing models of community that work in the increasing demands of adult life: family, career, church, and civic obligations. It's proving what faithfulness is in an increasingly fickle world. Secular man wants to know what will help him with reality.

How are we doing with reality? Here are a few questions that can move us beyond the pursuit of happiness to the pursuit of holiness:

- Why am I doing what I am doing? For "success"?
- What are my attitudes toward my family: parents, siblings, spouse, and children?
- Am I giving my work, my boss, and my colleagues my best, or am I just passing through or job-hopping?
- What are my civic obligations, and have I met them?
- Have I become a contributing member of a body of believers, or am I just a sideline critic?

Honest answers to these questions may keep us from falling into the trap of Cain. Refusing to answer up to God, even though Cain knew Him, he spent his life in uncommitted wandering, denying the implications of his own evasive question, "Am I my brother's keeper?" (Genesis 4:9).

From Prophets to Profits

"A bunch of stained-glass, gold-plated nonsense is what that is!" By this point in our conversation, my cabdriver had begun to portray his vehement disdain of all that had been of no help to him in this life.

"How is that?" I drew him out. I was beginning to see myself and the church that I loved in a different light. It was like looking at myself in the mirror right after getting out of bed in the morning—I wasn't quite ready to meet the public.

He went on and spoke of real needs. You couldn't fault his logic. Juvenile delinquency, drug abuse, lack of programs, and general public apathy; nothing escaped his practiced, cynical eye.

However, I wasn't going to let him put the last nails in my coffin without challenging him. So I asked him the big question, "What have *you* done about it?" Suddenly he was silent. But in his silence there was a certain amount of honesty. There was no self-justifying noise. Can we say the same?

As disciples are replaced by supporters, the authentic mark of a rough-hewn wooden cross somehow becomes gold-plated. Community and the sacrifice it entails gives way to a club. One pays his dues and comes and goes as he pleases—"the good life gospel." However, the watching world knows the club really isn't all that revolutionary. My cabdriver talked about his bowling club before I brought up the gospel.

Flushed with "success," have we abandoned the reality for the ritual? Tradition without genuine love will be challenged by secular man and will eventually be abandoned by its own children in search of reality.

Today's secular man is only a mirror, held in the hand of God, by which we can see ourselves as we really are. He reminds us how hard it is for some in the here and now to find genuine love amid the clanging cymbals of the counterfeits that surround us—among them, a Crossless Christianity.

Jonah refused to go to his "enemy" in Nineveh even when God himself had commanded it. Jonah had limited the borders of his love, and hence God's, to the frontiers of Israel and her ritual-filled Temple.

Later, when God showed himself merciful to Nineveh, Jonah sulked. It was simply beyond him that God could "so love" secular man. But that is what God is all about! He "so loves" and teaches us how in the process. "But I tell you: Love your enemies and pray for those who persecute you, that you may be sons of your Father in heaven" (Matthew 5:44-45).

That cabdriver is still there waiting and asking, "What earthly good is it?" Are we to wander like Cain in a private religious world that has no obligations? Or will we rebel like Jonah whenever we're asked to step outside of our comfortable religious subculture?

We have the warning of history.

As in Europe, America's believer-filled cathedrals will become tomorrow's empty museums unless we learn to see secular man as a bridge to greater authenticity in Christ. In meeting his honest needs as a friend, we purify ourselves and take up our crosses to follow Christ.

Geoff Gorsuch serves as a missionary for the Navigators in Grenoble, France.

Chapter 13

Building Bridges
in a World of Walls

by Jon Johnston

Background Scripture: James 2:1-4, 9; 1 Peter 2:5

SLUMPSTONE is a money-making industry in my home
state of California. People love it for building walls around
property. Unlike wooden or chain-link fences, slumpstone is
thick. It's perfect for sealing people off from their neighbors.

Behind slumpstone walls, people can hide and feel protected. And that's OK. But these walls also broadcast a pretty negative message to outsiders: *Come no farther.*

James Dobson, founder of Focus on the Family, said he saw a wall that made this message unmistakably clear. Attached to a wall surrounding a Santa Monica monastery was this sign:

ABSOLUTELY NO TRESPASSING. TRESPASSERS WILL BE PROSECUTED TO THE FULLEST EXTENT OF THE LAW.

The warning was signed, "Sisters of Mercy."

The whole world seems obsessed with wall building. In my travels, I've marveled at some famous ones.

For sheer beauty, my favorite is the blue-glazed, lion-etched wall of ancient Babylon—a section of which has been reconstructed in East Berlin's Pergamum Museum.

For most impressive, I'd have to cast my vote for China's Great Wall. Thirty-seven hundred miles long, it is wide enough on top for six horses to walk abreast. So massive it was seen by our astronauts on the moon.

To me, the most inspirational wall is Jerusalem's Wailing (or Western) Wall, built by King Herod. Small plants sprout between its cracks, along with thousands of prayer notes wedged there by devout Jews who come to the wall to pray. Its concrete blocks are massive—some weighing 60 tons. To most every Jew, this limestone wall represents the glory days of Israel's history.

Throughout the ages, humans have been building walls to protect themselves from one thing or another. But today we build them not so much to keep out wild animals or invading nations. We build them to protect our privacy. We build them with steel, wood, and stone. And we build some with invisible materials, harder to penetrate than anything we can touch.

Building Invisible Walls

Gloria Evans was a wall builder. She tells about it in her book *The Wall.*

> "One day I realized that [my] wall was so high that I no longer saw anybody go by. I no longer heard anyone. Everything was quiet. "Is there anyone there?" I yelled. There was no answer. It was dark inside the wall, and the air was foul. I sat there for a long time. It was quiet and dark and lonely.

Have you ever known wall builders who subjected themselves to such misery? I have.

A woman I know decided to build a bridge to some people. But she ended up building a wall. The unfortunate chain of events began at a church she used to attend. As a new member, she ventured out to become involved in a ladies' group. One of the women in the group was no lady. She was either very comfortable with the group as it existed, or she didn't like the guest. She told the visitor not to come back for the next meeting. And the visitor obliged. In fact, she refused to try building relationships with any other groups in the church.

Years later, after some of the sting from this rebuke had subsided, the woman began attending another church. Eventually, she convinced herself that her experience in the previous church was a fluke. It was time to stop the pity party and to begin building some bridges.

She tried. Would you believe it? Along came another woman, not exactly humming with mental health, who gave her a tongue-lashing. Former grievances and insecurities rushed to the surface. The hurt woman made an unfortunate decision: The cost of bridge building was too high.

As invariably occurs, once she decided this, wall construction began again. Even today, she refuses to attend any ladies' meetings.

My heart goes out to this wounded, tormented soul. She is no longer willing to pay the price of bridge building. Certainly there is a price, because there are risks. Rejection is one.

Reasons to Build Bridges

If only this woman would realize the price of building walls. These walls cut her off from enjoying the compassion of others and from sharing her own compassion. When this happens, we shrivel spiritually, as we turn inward and become increasingly fearful or selfish.

First Peter 2:5 says that as followers of Jesus, we are members of a "holy priesthood." Did you know that the Latin term for priest, or pontificate, literally means "bridge builder"? In a sense, the pope, or pontiff, is considered a bridge between God and humanity. Another similar bridge-builder word we're more familiar with is pontoon, a mobile bridge.

As God's bridge-building priests, we have an excellent model to follow.

Jesus built the most spectacular bridge of all time—one that extends from His Father in heaven all the way to us on earth.

Point established: Building bridges to others is our assignment, as members of the royal priesthood of God.

Sure, there are excuses for not giving the time, energy, and attention to building sturdy, reliable bridges to others.

• My job requires me to move a lot. It's emotionally exasperating to build bridges that, in a short while, must come crashing down.

But friendships can continue over distances.

• Past relationships have ended in anger, regret, or boredom. Who needs more disappointments?

To stop trying is to start dying. And painful lessons learned from the past can prepare us to build better relationships in the future.

• I'm just a naturally shy, withdrawn person. Why not go with my God-given natural temperament?

Undeniably, some people are more shy than others. But Stanford psychologist Philip G. Zimbardo says: Shyness is a disease that must be overcome—if we are to be mentally, emotionally, and even physically healthy *(Shyness: What It Is, What to Do About It)*.

Most of us want to be effective bridge builders. But many of us lack the strategies for doing what we want to do.

The Short Course on Bridge Building

Here are a few tips to keep in mind as we build bridges to a hurting world.

1. Show by our actions that the needs of others are at the top of our list of priorities.

We all know people who call only when they want something. And we know how this makes us feel. It's easy for us to fall into this pattern. Especially when our needs are great. And especially when our needs relate to God's work.

Nevertheless, we must avoid "sizing people up" to determine their potential for meeting our needs.

The ironic truth is that we often discover that meeting the needs of others is the best way to satisfy our own needs.

I remember hearing about a lost skier in a blinding Alaska snowstorm. He almost gave up. His arms and legs were already numb. But then he stumbled over a hard object—the collapsed body of another freezing person. Quickly he worked to bring the person back from the brink of death. As a result, not only did he save that person's life, but also he saved his own.

2. Stop imposing our agenda on others. Instead, focus on their interests.

A woman at my church spends a lot of time, effort, and

money training children for musical and drama productions. Many of these little ones come from unchurched homes.

During the weeks of rehearsals for "God's Kids" productions, parents previously not part of our church become intensely involved.

By tapping into their reservoir of interest (their children), this woman draws parents into the church.

The lesson is clear: We build strong bridges when we tap into the interests of others.

3. Consider elitism as an affront to our Lord, who ministered to all classes. Especially the lowly.

Our human nature sometimes causes us to gravitate to people who are active, verbal, intelligent, sociable, and financially comfortable. Perhaps this is because these people feed our vanity; they make us feel good about ourselves, and they draw other "successful" people to our churches. Some pastors I've known "wear" their people like badges.

In spite of this powerful temptation, our bridges must extend to all people. Especially to those who are disenfranchised and hurting.

James 2 says it all:

> My brothers, as believers in our glorious Lord Jesus Christ, don't show favoritism. Suppose a man comes into your meeting wearing a gold ring and fine clothes, and a poor man in shabby clothes also comes in. If you show special attention to the man wearing fine clothes and say, "Here's a good seat for you," but say to the poor man, "You stand there" or "Sit on the floor by my feet," have you not discriminated among yourselves and become judges with evil thoughts? . . . But if you show favoritism, you sin *(vv. 1-4, 9a)*.

That doesn't mean we should skip ministry to the talented, rich, powerful, beautiful people in our midst. It just means we should also minister to the rest of the world as well.

4. Develop strategies for building custom-made bridges to the four kinds of people we typically meet.

In the secular world, as well as in our churches, we will meet four kinds of people.

First, let's build footbridges to the devoted—our friends.

Footbridges, like the ornate ones that accent Japanese tea gardens, span tiny streams and picturesque dips in the terrain. This image seems to correspond with how we view our friends. To us, these loved ones are near and beautiful.

To build and maintain bridges to these people, we should:

• Believe the best, or at least give them the benefit of the doubt—unless we receive absolute, irrefutable evidence to the contrary.

• Neglect to neglect. These are the people we're quickest to take for granted, and slowest to express appreciation to.

Second, let's build drawbridges to the defiant.

Why drawbridges? Because they can be lowered when possible but retracted when necessary.

With these people, allow me to suggest two strategies:

• Approach them in an attitude of forgiveness. David Augsburger, a professor of pastoral psychology, says we should forgive immediately (after they hurt us). And we must forgive continually.

• When confronting these people, we should speak the truth in love (Ephesians 4:15). This allows us to solve problems and seek the defiant person's best interests.

Third, let's build causeways to the different.

Causeways that connect the Florida Keys extend long distances and float—to insure flexibility. When reaching out to the different in our midst (social klutzes, dropouts, handicapped, ethnic minorities, all who differ from the majority mainstream), we should reach far and be very flexible.

We do this most effectively when we stop thinking hierarchically. All are equally valuable. Jesus died for each of us.

Remembering that is essential in becoming "one in the bond of love."

Reaching far means going beyond just trying to be nice. Mere saccharine smiles, backslaps, and glad-handing tells them they're being processed—as when they shop for a car. Niceness isn't enough. It must be accompanied by full, no-holds-barred acceptance.

Finally, let's build covered bridges to the distant.

Perhaps these are the hardest ones of all to reach. They send clear signals that they don't care about us or our message. They are tuned out and turned off.

Why covered bridges? Because they suggest closeness, warmth, and intimacy.

Without being pushy, we must somehow invade the protective shells of these people with the love of Jesus. They need warmth, acceptance, and understanding. And they need these without strings attached.

I think we can begin helping these people overcome their emotional numbness when we involve them in activities that address their needs and interests.

Why bother with any of this?

Because, if we're committed to Jesus, we are committed to others in His name. And that means bridge building. Even when privacy is the rage and slumpstone sales are soaring. And even when it's costly and inconvenient—which is most of the time.

Jon Johnston is a professor of sociology at Pepperdine University, Malibu, Calif. He has adapted this chapter from his book *Walls or Bridges: How to Build Relationships that Glorify God* (Baker).

Other Dialog Series Books

Christian Personality Under Construction
Christians at Work in a Hurting World
Christians in a Crooked World
Coping with Traumas of Family Life
Growing Season—Maturing of a Christian
How to Improve Your Prayer Life
How to Live the Holy Life
Less Stress, Please
Misguiding Lights?
No Easy Answers
Questions You Shouldn't Ask About Christianity
Questions You Shouldn't Ask About the Church
Raising Kids
Spiritual Zest
Timeless Truths for Timely Living
Tough Questions—Christian Answers
Turning Points
What Jesus Said About. . .
When Life Gets Rough

For a description of all available Dialog Series books, including some that may not be listed here, contact your local bookstore or your publishing house and ask for the free Dialog Series brochure.